PRAISE FOR STUDENT VOICE: TURN UP T̶
6–12 ACTIVITY BOOK BY RUSSELL J. Q
MICHAEL J. CORSO, AND JULIE HELLERS̶T̶E̶I̶N̶

This activity book will captivate your students through meaningful and exciting social building events. It will not be gathering dust in your resource collection. It will be one of the first you grab to develop excitement and the voice of your students. It puts fun in building life skills while meeting the ASCA standards.

—**Don Acker Sr.**, School Counselor

Engaging, insightful, and creative, this activity book provides rich tools through which students and teachers can learn about, practice, and apply the authors' principles in meaningful ways. Embedded with standards-based best practice strategies and a variety of technology applications, the activities offer an array of deeper learning experiences in a format that can be personalized for any classroom or group of students. *Turn Up the Volume* ensures a classroom environment in which student voice is valued and student aspirations are the focus.

—**Beth Havens**, Horry County Professional Development

This activity book is a teacher's dream! It is more than clear that the authors actually talked to teachers in the creation of this resource, which has it all: data-driven content, group discussions, engaging student activities, personal reflection and extension opportunities, connections to technology, AND designed for flexible use to meet the needs of individual teachers. Incredible, and a MUST-HAVE for every K–8 teacher!

—**Dr. Lisa L. Lande**, Executive Director of the Teacher Voice & Aspirations International Center

Teachers are not the only leaders in the classroom. Quaglia, Corso, and Hellerstein emphasize that any person who participates in the process of learning has a voice that should be engaged in schools. This book provides a plethora of opportunities for students to influence learning, take ownership, and develop a sense of worth and belonging in the classroom. Each activity was created and designed to guide students to be determined and goal oriented, while inspiring them to establish and work toward their future goals in school and life. This brilliant book showcases what seemed to be the impossible—a collaborative connection between students' active engagement and emotional involvement in their schoolwork, while linked to the Common Core Standards, 21st Century Skills, and International Society for Technology in Education (ISTE) requirements.

—**Tiffany Lewis**, First-Grade Teacher

The authors have once again designed an extraordinary road map for teachers to use in guiding students to find their true voice. A research-based road map, yes, but more important, a map teachers can use to guide students to find their voice through their experiences. The wonderful activities herein are inspiring, engaging, and interactive and ultimately lead students to discover their own unique voice and aspirations!

—**Rich McBride,** President and Executive Director, AESA

Partner the *Student Voice Activity Books* with the foundational book, *Student Voice: The Instrument of Change*, and the secret to turning schools and classrooms into vibrant communities of engaged learners will be revealed. Quaglia, Corso, and Hellerstein have masterfully woven together a practical and relevant fabric of activities that reinforces for students the importance of relationships, active and engaging teaching and learning, and exercising a sense of responsibility over one's own goals. Thanks to these authors, we now have a compendium of strategies designed to give students a meaningful voice in the educational process.

—**Dr. Raymond L. Smith,** Author of *School Improvement for the Next Generation* and *Evaluating Instructional Leadership*

One of the few books on education in the last several decades that has a touch of genius, this book gives teachers strategies that help them build and nurture relationships with their students and make learning more engaging and relevant to students' lives—resulting in higher levels of student achievement. The authors provide proven strategies and impart skills—connected to Common Core Standards, 21st Century, and ISTE requirements—that can be immediately applied to positively impact every student, teacher, and school leader in America.

—**Dr. Julie R. Smith,** Author of *Evaluating Instructional Leadership*

AVAILABLE FROM CORWIN
ISBN: 978-1-4833-5813-0

Student Voice

Turn Up the Volume
6–12 Activity Book

Russell J. Quaglia

Michael J. Corso

Julie Hellerstein

CORWIN
A SAGE Company

FOR INFORMATION:

Corwin
A SAGE Company
2455 Teller Road
Thousand Oaks, California 91320
(800) 233-9936
www.corwin.com

SAGE Publications Ltd.
1 Oliver's Yard
55 City Road
London EC1Y 1SP
United Kingdom

SAGE Publications India Pvt. Ltd.
B 1/I 1 Mohan Cooperative Industrial Area
Mathura Road, New Delhi 110 044
India

SAGE Publications Asia-Pacific Pte. Ltd.
3 Church Street
#10-04 Samsung Hub
Singapore 049483

Executive Editor: Arnis Burvikovs
Senior Associate Editor: Desirée A. Bartlett
Editorial Assistant: Andrew Olson
Production Editor: Melanie Birdsall
Copy Editor: Diane DiMura
Typesetter: C&M Digitals (P) Ltd.
Proofreader: Laura Webb
Indexer: Wendy Allex
Cover Designer: Candice Harman
Marketing Manager: Lisa Lysne

Printed in the United States of America

ISBN 978-1-4833-8274-6

This book is printed on acid-free paper.

15 16 17 18 19 10 9 8 7 6 5 4 3 2 1

Contents

PREFACE: NO ORDINARY ACTIVITY BOOK — ix

ACKNOWLEDGMENTS — xvii

ABOUT THE AUTHORS — xix

CHAPTER 1: BELONGING — 1

Grades 9-12: Belonging Activities
Aspirations Story Squares — 3
Odd Dot Out — 7
Inside/Outside — 10

Grades 6-8: Belonging Activities
Pick a Number — 12
All About Me Cloud and Class Cloud — 16
Belong-Meme — 18

CHAPTER 2: HEROES — 20

Grades 9-12: Heroes Activities
Breaking News — 22
Heroes Here in the Classroom — 24
Heroes-Based Learning — 27

Grades 6-8: Heroes Activities
I Can Be a Hero Poem — 29
Utilizing YOU! — 31
Gratitude — 33

CHAPTER 3: SENSE OF ACCOMPLISHMENT — 35

Grades 9-12: Sense of Accomplishment Activities
Scholarship — 37
What About the Rest of the Alphabet? — 39
Snapshot Show and Tell — 41

Grades 6-8: Sense of Accomplishment Activities
Marble Roll — 43
Student Actions — 45
Headline News — 49

CHAPTER 4: FUN & EXCITEMENT   52

Grades 9-12: Fun & Excitement Activities
Tweet Teach   54

Menu   56

Learning That Sticks   59

Grades 6-8: Fun & Excitement Activities
Heads Up!   61

Appy Hour   63

Un-Bored Games   65

CHAPTER 5: CURIOSITY & CREATIVITY   67

Grades 9-12: Curiosity & Creativity Activities
Blackout Poetry   69

Genius Hour/Passion Project   72

Why Do We Need to Learn This?   75

Grades 6-8: Curiosity & Creativity Activities
Quick Question   77

The Curiosity Convention   79

Marshmallow Challenge   81

CHAPTER 6: SPIRIT OF ADVENTURE   83

Grades 9-12: Spirit of Adventure Activities
Student-Led Help Desk   85

In the Zone   87

I Dare You Cards   89

Grades 6-8: Spirit of Adventure Activities
Student Speak   91

Adventure Advice   93

Never Lose Sight of Your Goal   95

CHAPTER 7: LEADERSHIP & RESPONSIBILITY   97

Grades 9-12: Leadership & Responsibility Activities
Scholarship Situations   99

School Solutions   102

Good, Bad, Horrible Advice   105

Grades 6-8: Leadership & Responsibility Activities
Tag Team Debate   108

Drawing Dictations   110

Values Auction   112

CHAPTER 8: CONFIDENCE TO TAKE ACTION   115

Grades 9-12: Confidence to Take Action Activities
From There to Here   117

Linked-In Learning   121

Cool, Calm, and Confident Collage   124

Grades 6-8: Confidence to Take Action Activities

    Time Capsule   126

    Extreme Community Makeover   129

    Letter to the Editor   131

APPENDIX A: COMMON CORE STATE STANDARDS, GRADES 6–12   133

APPENDIX B: PARTNERSHIP FOR 21ST CENTURY SKILLS, GRADES 6–12   135

APPENDIX C: ISTE STANDARDS, GRADES 6–12   136

INDEX   138

To the students and staff who inspire and challenge us to always have high aspirations.
You are constant reminders that there is no age requirement to improve
the teaching and learning environment!

Preface:
No Ordinary Activity Book

You cannot always judge a book by its subtitle. Take this book, for instance. It is less about the activities and more about the experience. It is designed to involve and inspire teachers and students. This book is both research- and need-based—designed to bring together sound practice with what teachers and students want and need to create an engaging learning environment that fosters students' aspirations.

The authors bring to this book critical professional knowledge, beliefs, and first-hand experiences in this field:

- extensive knowledge of over thirty years of research on student aspirations;
- involvement with teachers and students in Grades K–12 throughout the academic year, talking with and, most importantly, listening to them;
- belief that students have something to teach us and every interaction is an opportunity to learn from students; and
- belief in a nonscripted approach to education, therefore never *telling* you what to do, rather, focusing on providing inspiring ideas for you to breathe life into.

You know your students best, not to mention they know themselves. Our goal is to provide a tool that you can utilize and adapt to meet the needs of your students. We hope and expect that you will integrate your professional knowledge with the knowledge of your students to bring this activity book alive.

Our background and beliefs are important, but this book is not just the result of our collective wisdom—it's the result of yours. We spoke with hundreds of teachers and asked them what they would value in an activity book. Their top ten wishes were to make sure that

- each activity is simple to implement, yet complex enough to keep students engaged;
- activities are age appropriate and can be used with groups of students with mixed abilities;
- activities are adaptive and can be personalized, but are also generalizable;
- students can lead the activities;
- activities can be used in a wide range of contexts (in class and outside of school);

- activities do not cost money;
- activities can delve into "deeper learning" if teachers want to extend into richer investigations with students;
- activities are connected to our mandated curricula and standards;
- activities can be understood by parents or guardians at home; and
- activities are not a waste of my time!

Tall orders indeed, but we asked because we wanted to know. We believe in the value of listening to, learning from, and responding to the teachers and students who are involved in the educational environment every day–those who inform and are directly impacted by the work we do.

What have we learned? That when activities are too complex, they become scripted rather than organic, and do not promote spontaneity or deeper learning. On the flip side, when activities are too simple, they become bland and unproductive. In response, we took great care to maintain flexibility in the activities, allowing for teachers to connect an individual's skill with the challenges presented. Did we get it right 100% of the time? Certainly not—that's an inherently impossible task. No two teachers, classrooms, or students are alike. Your expertise and knowledge of your students will allow you to create the experience that is right for your classes.

It's critical that when students work in groups, they still recognize their individual "print" on each activity, that no individual become camouflaged within the group. Therefore, we developed activities that involve the entire class, while simultaneously meeting the individual student's needs.

Our work is based on the belief students have something to teach us. Thus, many of the activities do not have a defined ending. The ending should emerge with and be determined by each group. For example, some activities could take ten minutes, while others could take up to a week depending on how much deeper you want to take that specific learning. Each activity has an estimated time for completion, but again, it is not up to us to tell you how much or how little time you should spend on any one activity. It is dependent on you, your students, and the circumstances of the moment.

It would also be naive for us to tell you what time of year to offer various activities. That is very personal and circumstantial. For example in the beginning of the year, you may want to spend more time on Belonging activities; if you are working with a group of students that want to take their leadership to the next level, we would suggest the Confidence to Take Action activities; if the class seems flat, you should introduce activities driven by Spirit of Adventure or Fun & Excitement. The bottom line is that student groups will take activities to levels beyond what we imagined, while other activities will not have the desired impact on some groups. Throughout it all, please keep in mind—teachers are not the only leaders in the classroom. We suggest that students be provided opportunities to organize and implement the activities. This approach, in and of itself, will increase engagement in the classroom.

We promise this book is unlike any you have seen before. The activities are engaging, meaningful, and relevant to your students. They can be accomplished with virtually no financial implications, and while they are connected to school, they are not restricted to school. Each activity can stand alone and be implemented outside of the school setting. We made it a point to ensure that ALL activities are connected to Common Core Standards (CCSS), 21st Century Skills, and International Society for Technology in Education (ISTE) requirements. Activities include personal reflections, group reflections, and extended learning opportunities. For Personal Reflection, have students select one or more of the prompts and write a journal entry, a poem, or song lyrics to share on a class blog or website. Use your own questions as well to generate a conversation about the activity. The Extended Learning sections are opportunities to continue the learning.

Why bring this all together in one book? We know it's important, and we know time is precious in schools . . . for students and teachers.

Alongside teachers' beliefs in taking the time to develop relationships and make learning engaging and relevant to students' lives, we realize teachers are accountable for ensuring a myriad of standards are met. They do this all on a fixed budget within a fixed amount of time. This book will not magically add hours to your day, but it is designed to help you maximize the time you do have with your students. All three authors have been teachers (and in multifaceted ways, still are). We know firsthand the challenges of the fixed resource of time. In and of themselves, these activities are a productive use of time. When done well, they will open up doors for extended learning, resulting in even more engaged learning in important content areas.

This book would not be complete if we did not ask students what is useful for them. We did. Not surprisingly, many responses were similar to those of their teachers. However, there were two distinct themes that were frequently echoed by students: *I want activities that are about ME!* and *The activities need to be fun.* Regardless of age—kindergarteners through seniors—students felt strongly that learning should be fun, with one student making an important distinction: "I want to be engaged, not entertained."

The feedback from students reinforced what we knew–that the activities need to be rooted in the very fabric of what guides our work each and every day: putting into practice the conditions that foster student aspirations. In order for teachers and students to work together in a manner where students' can realize their potential, the activities need to be grounded in research and a theoretical Aspirations Framework.

We define Aspirations as *the ability to dream and set goals for the future, while being inspired in the present to reach those dreams.* To understand, work toward, and achieve one's aspirations, there must be a future and present component. Aspirations are about *dreaming* of the future and *doing* in the present; combining the vision of what we want to achieve with the willingness to do what is necessary now to make that dream a reality.

In order to help schools and educators foster student aspirations, Drs. Quaglia and Corso have developed the Aspirations Profile, a visual model of behaviors that support and hinder success. The Aspirations Profile has two dimensions: Dreaming and Doing.

We can look at Aspirations graphically if we think of each aspect—present/doing and future/dreaming—as the X- and Y-axis of a grid.

ASPIRATIONS PROFILE

	Imagination	**Aspirations**
High	Sets goals for the future but does not put forth the effort to reach those goals.	Sets goals for future and puts forth effort in the present to reach those goals.
Future/Dreaming	**Hibernation** Has no goals for the future and puts no effort in the present.	**Perspiration** Works hard in the present but has no goals for the future.
Low	**Present/Doing**	**High**

Source: Adapted from Quaglia and Corso, *Student Voice: The Instrument of Change* (2014).

Seen this way, the two aspects of the definition provide us with four categories:

Hibernation

Students in the Hibernation category do not think about the future, have no clear goals, and put forth no effort in daily life. Those in hibernation are stalled—they have neither a picture of where they want to go, nor the energy for doing much in the present. Such people lack a sense of purpose and rarely experience a sense of accomplishment in anything they do.

Perspiration

Perspiration is the category that describes someone who works exceptionally hard, always puts forth effort, but lacks direction or purpose. Such people are diligent, but directionless; they are often busy but see no meaningful future in front of them.

Imagination

Students in the category of Imagination readily share their future plans but show little, if any, effort to reach those dreams. These individuals have positive attitudes about their prospects but take no steps in the present to achieve their goals.

Aspirations

Students with Aspirations are determined and goal oriented. With genuine aspirations comes the clear vision of a future destination, and the passion for exerting oneself in the present to reach that destination. Such people have the ability to set goals for themselves and are inspired to work toward those goals *now*. They have a vision about what they want to do and who they want to become. They commit the energy, time, and resources required to meet their objectives.

The neat quadrants of the Aspirations Profile betray an obvious fact: Our aspirations operate on a dynamic continuum, more so than in a static set of boxes. Students may be in hibernation as they mindlessly recover in front of a television show after a long day at school, but that is not their permanent state. They may be in perspiration temporarily because you have given them an important task and they do not yet have a clear picture of how it fits in with their learning. A student who has been procrastinating on an assignment may fall into the imagination state, contemplating how nice it would be to get high praise for the work, knowing she has not put in the required effort. All students are not aspiring all the time. Yet, when they are, their full potential comes into focus. Students are not fully engaged when they are dozing or daydreaming or participating out of sheer duty. Students are revealing and realizing their full potential when they are taking action to bring about the goals they have set for themselves—a process of becoming who, not just what, they want to be.

The activities in this book are designed to guide students into the upper right quadrant of the Aspirations Profile, inspiring them in the present to establish and work toward their future goals—in school and life.

The Aspirations Profile unfolds in the Aspirations Framework, which outlines a way to recognize and develop students' aspirations. The Framework is based on Dr. Quaglia's 3 Guiding Principles that show up consistently in research and are at the core of what motivates students to achieve their dreams. We believe the 3 Guiding Principles must be present for students to have high aspirations.

GUIDING PRINCIPLES

The 3 Guiding Principles that support students' aspirations are:

Self-Worth

Self-Worth occurs when students know they are uniquely valued members of the school community; they have a person in their lives they can trust and learn from; and they believe they have the ability to achieve—academically, personally and socially. With Self-Worth, students are more likely to persevere through difficult tasks and stake the steps needed to reach their goals.

Engagement

Engagement occurs when students are deeply involved in the learning process as characterized by enthusiasm, a desire to learn new things, and a willingness to take positive, healthy steps toward the future. Students are meaningfully engaged when they are emotionally, intellectually, and behaviorally invested in learning. With Engagement, learning—and therefore participation in learning—becomes important in and of itself.

Purpose

Purpose exists when students take responsibility for *who* and *what* they want to become. Students need to explore what it means to have, and create, a successful and rewarding life. This is about more than deciding on a career. It is about becoming an involved, responsible member of the community and making choices that lead to a meaningful, productive, and rewarding life.

The Guiding Principles are lived out through 8 Conditions that emphasize relationships, active and engaging teaching and learning, and a sense of responsibility over one's own goals. We refer to these as the 8 Conditions That Make a Difference™ in our 2003 book, *Raising Student Aspirations: Eight Conditions That Make a Difference.*

8 CONDITIONS IN SCHOOL

Teachers create *Self-Worth* in the classroom when they foster these three Conditions:

Belonging: The belief that a student is a valued member of a community, while still allowing the student to maintain his or her uniqueness. By creating a sense of belonging, teachers foster students' self-confidence and investment in the community.

Heroes: The everyday people in students' lives who inspire them to excel and to make positive changes in attitudes and lifestyles. Teachers have prime opportunities to be Heroes to their students. Building relationships with students through support, guidance, and encouragement enables them to become more confident in their academic, personal, and social growth.

Sense of Accomplishment: The recognition of effort, perseverance, and citizenship—along with academic achievement—as signs of student success. When teachers take time to recognize and support students' efforts, it can help motivate them to persevere through challenges, creating an appreciation for hard work and dedication.

Teachers create *Engagement* for students when they are purposeful about creating lessons that instill the following Conditions:

Fun & Excitement: Students' active engagement and emotional involvement in their schoolwork. To foster Fun & Excitement in school, teachers can offer students new opportunities, as well as meaningful challenges, that are connected with their individual interests.

Curiosity & Creativity: Inquisitiveness, eagerness, a strong desire to learn and develop new or interesting things, and a longing to satisfy the mind with new discoveries. To sustain student motivation, teachers can devote extra attention to creating learning environments that promote questioning and creative exploration.

Spirit of Adventure: Students' ability to take on positive, healthy challenges at school and home, with family and friends. When teachers promote healthy decision making and healthy risk taking, students can become more confident and resilient.

Finally, teachers create a sense of *Purpose* for students by promoting the Conditions of:

Leadership & Responsibility: Students being able to express their ideas, make decisions, and show a willingness to be accountable for their actions. When teachers foster leadership, students become empowered to make just and appropriate decisions, take pride in their actions, and accept accountability for their choices.

Confidence to Take Action: The extent to which students believe in themselves and act in pursuit of their goals. Teachers can help build their students' Confidence to Take Action by having high expectations of students, providing support, and encouraging independent thinking.

The activities in the book are organized around the 3 Guiding Principles and the 8 Conditions that affect student aspirations. It would be naive of us, and misleading, if we claimed these activities would make your life "easier" as a teacher. We can promise, however, that they will add a dimension to your teaching—one that enhances the learning environment for all by supporting the conditions that foster student aspirations. These activities are a venue through which students can use *their voice* to express themselves—their opinions, their values, their hopes and dreams. These activities promote a learning environment that is driven by interest, relevance, and engagement. As you and your students breathe your own life into these activities, connections will be made to the Common Core, and a dimension of realism will be added to 21st Century Skills. You will capitalize on technology, promote interdisciplinary connections, and engage students in practical, meaningful, and productive ways. (Maybe it does make your teaching life "easier" after all!)

Aspire . . . Dream big. Act now. Commit to showing your students, and yourself, that this is unlike any other activity book you've seen before. These are not merely activities—they're experiences waiting to happen.

Group Reflection:

- What did you learn about your classmates? How did they make their story meaningful to you?
- How does knowing your classmates' stories benefit our class as a whole?
- Why is it important to interact with all different types of students?
- Why is it important for your teachers to know you as an individual? How could this help you be successful?
- What was it like to share your story squares? What details are necessary to explain to someone when creating a narrative?
- What will help orient or engage your audience to your narrative?

Extended Learning:

Using a smartphone or tablet, students can create their Aspirations Squares using a photo collage app like Pic Stitch. Have students select an eight-frame template or make two, four-frame templates. Students can use their own personal photographs or images from the Web or photo gallery.

Students can record their narratives and create a podcast using Apple's Podcasts app, InstaCast4, Downcast, GarageBand or podcast tool of your choice.

Notes:

_____

_____

_____

_____

_____

_____

_____

_____

_____

Name _____

1. Draw or write something that makes you special or unique.	2. Draw a picture or write the name of someone who is there for you when you need them.
3. Draw a picture of an accomplishment you are proud of other than your grades.	4. Draw a picture or briefly describe how you learn best.
5. Write down a question you would like to know the answer to or a topic you are curious about.	6. Write down something you would like to try, but you are not sure if you will be good at it.
7. Draw a picture of when you have been a leader.	8. Write down something you would like to do in the future and how you could start achieving this goal today.

Odd Dot Out

(ABOUT 50 MINUTES)

Belonging:

Feeling like you are part of a group while knowing you are special for who you are.

Objective:

Students will be able to empathize with others who do not feel accepted or valued. In this activity, students will experience the relief of being part of a group or the loneliness associated with being excluded.

Materials:

Colored sticker dots (or any other kind of small, varied stickers).

Steps:

- Before the activity buy enough colored dot stickers for the size of your class to form several groups of four or five plus one unique color dot. For example, if you have twenty students you will need: five red dots, five green dots, five blue dots, four orange dots, and one yellow dot.

- Place dots on students' foreheads without allowing them to see the color. Tell them not to indicate what color another student is receiving. Make sure you put the lone sticker on a student who can handle being left out, but also a student who will express that it does not feel good to be left out.

- Inform students that they may not speak once the activity starts.

- Next, tell students they must get into groups based on the color sticker on their forehead without talking. Create a sense of urgency by telling students the activity should not be taking as long as it is and suggesting everyone should have a group. Instruct the students to huddle together once they have found their group.

- All students will eventually find their group after being rejected a few times. The student who has the sticker that does not match any group will likely not be accepted into any group and end up standing alone.

- Have students remain standing in their groups and begin a discussion on belonging, exclusion, and cliques using the following group discussion questions.

> **Common Core:**
> CCSS.ELA-LITERACY.W.9-10.6
> Use technology, including the Internet, to produce, publish, and update individual or shared writing products, taking advantage of technology's capacity to link to other information and to display information flexibly and dynamically.
>
> **21st Century Skills:**
> Critical Thinking and Problem Solving, Communication and Collaboration, Information, Media, and Technology Skills
>
> **ISTE/NETS:**
> Communication and collaboration A, B, D
> Critical thinking, problem solving, and decision making A

Source: Photo by Julie Hellerstein.

Personal Assessment:

Have students return to their seats and take out a piece of paper and number it from 1 to 8. Tell them to score themselves for each of the following statements using the following scale: 4 Always, 3 Most of the time, 2 Sometimes, 1 Rarely, 0 Never. Put the scale on the board if it would be helpful.

1. I am comfortable being myself at school.

2. I understand others' viewpoints and ideas.

3. I interact with all different types of students.

4. I don't rush to judge other students' actions.

5. I support peers who have trouble fitting in at school.

6. I share my ideas and opinions in class.

7. I make sure my teachers know me as an individual.

8. I do not bully other students at school.

After scoring each statement, have students pick one of the statements and provide evidence for why they gave the score they did.

Personal Reflection:

- How do you support peers who have trouble fitting in?
- Do cliques increase a students' sense of Belonging or decrease a sense of Belonging? Explain.
- How can we be more accepting and tolerant of differences? Give personal examples of how you accept differences.
- When have you been accepted for your uniqueness? Explain how it made you feel.
- Should students conform and lose their uniqueness to be part of a group?
- What makes you special and unique? How do you embrace it?

Group Discussion:

- Why did you form your group with others who had the same color dot?
- Could you have created heterogeneous groups? (Note that the instructions asked students to get into groups based on the color on their forehead, not based on *like* colors.)
- Why does it seem natural to group yourself with others who are like you?
- What benefits are there to being around people who are different from you?
- Ask the student who had the lone dot sticker to share his or her experience.
- Are students excluded at school? Give examples.
- How does it feel to be left out versus accepted? How did it feel when you were with your group?
- What is the difference between a clique and a friendship group? (Cliques are not permeable, hard to enter and leave. Friendship groups are open.)
- Explore ways to demonstrate acceptance in the classroom and at school.

Extended Learning:

Record the Odd Dot Out experience. Have students edit the video and create an iMovie about Belonging to share with their peers.

Inside/Outside

(ABOUT 50 MINUTES)

Belonging:

Feeling like you are part of a group while knowing you are special for who you are.

Objective:

Students will be able to create a visual representation of how they believe others see them and how they see themselves.

Materials:

Brown paper bags; small pieces of paper; markers.

Steps:

- Have students decorate a brown paper bag with words that describe how they believe others see them (e.g., loud, class clown, football player).

- Invite students to write down characteristics of who they really are on slips of paper and put them inside the brown paper bag. Encourage students to write down information that their classmates may not know. Each student should write at least three characteristics.

- Ask students to sit in a circle and place the bag so that others can read the words on the outside of the bag.

- Next have students pull out the slips of paper and read aloud who they are on the inside. Each person should read one at a time.

Personal Reflection:

Instruct students to write an advice column for other students. They should answer the question: How can we be more accepting of others and stop judging others before we get to know them? Encourage them to include tips on how students can really get to know someone. Suggest they share an experience when they were judged or labeled before or when they have judged someone else.

Group Discussion:

- Ask students if they discovered something in common with a classmate that they were not aware of. Share examples.

- In small groups, have students discuss what happens when students judge other students without really knowing each other. Do we make judgments about someone before we really get to know them? Why do we do this? Give examples.

- In small groups, ask students to brainstorm how students can be more accepting and tolerant of others. One representative from each group should share their ideas to the large group.

Extended Learning:

Students will create a Flipagram video starting with the outside of their bag and flashing to the statements on the inside. Students can incorporate other pictures to help tell their story.

Source: Photo by Julie Hellerstein

Notes:

_____

_____

_____

_____

_____

Pick a Number

(30–40 MINUTES)

Common Core:

Comprehension and Collaboration:

CCSS.ELA-LITERACY.SL.6.1, 7.1, 8.1 Engage effectively in a range of collaborative discussions (one-on-one, in groups, and teacher-led) with diverse partners on grade 6, 7, 8 topics, texts, and issues, building on others' ideas and expressing their own clearly.

21st Century Skills:

Communication and Collaboration, Critical Thinking and Problem Solving

ISTE/NETS:

Creativity and innovation B

Belonging:

Feeling like you are part of a group while knowing you are special for who you are.

Objective:

Students will be able to ask their classmates questions and engage in dialogue with their peers.

Materials:

List of questions for each group; number spinner available at http://www.classtools.net/random-name-picker/37_jk2H7U.

Steps:

- Instruct students to break up into groups of eight to ten. Give each group the list of questions on the next page. One person in the group will be assigned as the question asker but should also answer a question, too.

- Have each student choose two numbers by spinning the random picker wheel or by verbally choosing a number. These numbers will correspond to questions on the next page.

- Each student will answer his or her two questions. As a teacher, you should answer some questions, too.

- Have students share one number with the questioner who will read the question they have been assigned. After answering the first round of questions, the exercise should be repeated to answer the second question.

Questions

1. What is something you think that should be taught in school that currently isn't?

2. What Disney character would you want to be your best friend?

3. What is your favorite food?

4. If you could travel anywhere, where would it be?

5. If you could be an animal, which one would you be? Why?

6. What can you teach me?

7. What is your favorite sports team?

8. What chores do you have to do at home?

9. Do you have any pets? If not, what pet would you like to have?

10. When is school fun for you?

11. When are you at your most creative?

12. Who is your role model?

13. When do you take healthy risks at school? For example, do you try something even if you do not know if you will be good at it.

14. Describe the current state of your room. Is your room messy or clean?

15. Who do you think is the most successful person alive today? Explain.

16. What is your favorite school supply?

17. Do you have any nicknames? Who gave them to you?

18. What is the best book you have read?

19. What is your biggest win or success of the week?

20. Are you an early bird or a night owl?

21. What is your most challenging school subject?

22. What is your favorite childhood toy?

23. What talent would you really like to have?

24. Would you rather play in a pool or the snow?

Continued

Continued

25. What is your birthday?

26. What is your lucky or favorite number? Why?

27. Name a quote or song lyric that describes your life.

28. There is a movie being made about you. What actor or actress should play you?

29. What state do you think you should actually live in?

30. What is your favorite day of the week? Explain.

31. What is the best thing about going to this school?

32. What is your favorite lunch food?

33. What is one thing you would change about school?

34. How many siblings do you have? How many cousins?

35. What is your favorite TV show?

36. What is your favorite app?

37. What is the best thing someone has ever done for you?

38. What is your pet peeve? What annoys you?

39. Who has influenced you the most this past year?

40. What qualities make an effective teacher?

41. What is something nice that you have done for someone else?

42. What TV, book, or movie character is most like you?

43. What foreign country would you like to live in?

44. Describe one of your favorite school projects.

45. What is your favorite dessert?

46. What is your idea of the perfect weekend?

47. Who is your favorite musician?

48. What language would you like to learn?

49. What do you do in your spare time?

50. What song could you listen to on repeat? Why?

Personal Reflection:

Have students reflect on the activity and prepare ideas that they will share in the group activity.

- Ask: Why is it important for us to get to know each other? How does this impact your experience in this class? How does it impact your learning?
- Explain: Although we are all individuals, we also belong to one class. We need to respect each individual in our classroom community.
- Ask: How can we achieve this? What does a classroom community look like? What actions do students need to take?

Group Activity:

- As a class, come up with a class rule that all students agree to follow that reflects the importance of classroom community. Students must collaborate with each other and with the teacher to create this rule. Post the rule in your classroom and on the class website.

Extended Learning:

Option 1: Have students work in small groups to form their own questions. Play another time with student created questions. Or repeat with the questions provided by having students choose new numbers.

Option 2: Students will create a getting to know you questionnaire on Google forms or another simple quiz or survey creator tool. Have students partner up and answer each other's questions. For quiz tools, go to http://www.teachthought.com/technology/35-digital-tools-create-simple-quizzes-collect-feedback-students/.

Notes:

_____

_____

_____

_____

_____

_____

All About Me Cloud and Class Cloud

(ABOUT 50 MINUTES)

Common Core:
CCSS.ELA-LITERACY.W.6.6, 7.6, 8.6
Use technology, including the Internet, to produce and publish writing and link to and cite sources as well as to interact and collaborate with others, including linking to and citing sources.

21st Century Skills:
Communication and Collaboration, Information, Communications and Technology Literacy

ISTE/NETS:
Creativity and innovation A, B, D

Belonging:

Feeling like you are part of a group while knowing you are special for who you are.

Objective:

Students will be able to create a personalized word cloud and contribute to a collaborative class word cloud. Students will be able to identify similarities and predict trends.

Materials:

Access to computers, Wordsalad or another word cloud generator; visit http://www.educatorstechnology.com/2013/09/6-great-apps-to-create-word-clouds-on.html.

Steps:

- Have students brainstorm a list of words including their interests, future goals, and personality characteristics.

- Direct them to the Wordsalad app. This tool generates a word cloud from text that students provide. Students will edit the shape, the direction of the words, and the colors to personalize their world clouds.

- To start, students will click the plus sign in the corner and begin building their cloud. Students will enter words and click start. Next, students can edit the format. Students can export their images to save or share.

- Next, ask students to generate a list of words to describe the class as a group. Tell them to get creative. Have them define the goals, attributes, and personality of your class. Everyone should contribute to a list.

- Then create a class word cloud using all the students' input.
- Before printing or posting the word cloud, have students predict what the common trends in this word cloud will be. The trending words will appear larger in the word cloud.

Personal Reflection:

Have students choose three words in their personal word clouds and reflect on why they picked these words. Ask: What do these words mean to you? Suggest that in their explanation, they include links to relevant websites for classmates to learn more about their interests, values, or personal characteristics. Share this on a class Edmodo page, social media page, or class blog.

Source: Created using Wordsalad.

Group Discussion:

Why is it important to acknowledge and embrace both similarities and differences?

Extended Learning:

Option 1: Have students post their word clouds to Edmodo, a class blog, or class Twitter account.

Option 2: Have students help you create a bulletin board in your classroom displaying the word clouds.

Notes:

_____

_____

_____

_____

_____

_____

Belong-Meme

(ABOUT 50 MINUTES)

Common Core:
CCSS.ELA-LITERACY.CCRA.W.4
Produce clear and coherent writing in which the development, organization, and style are appropriate to task, purpose, and audience.

CCSS.ELA-LITERACY.CCRA.W.6
Use technology, including the Internet, to produce and publish writing and to interact and collaborate with others.

21st Century Skills:
Communication and Collaboration, Information, Communications and Technology Literacy

ISTE/NETS:
Creativity and innovation A, B, C, D
Communication and collaboration A, B, C, D

Research and fluency A, B, C, D

Critical thinking, problem solving, and decision making A, B, C, D

Digital citizenship B
Technology operations and concepts A, D

Belonging:

Feeling like you are part of a group while knowing you are special for who you are. Your uniqueness and individuality is what makes you a special and important part of the school. It is important for you to feel a sense of Belonging in order to be truly who you are and who you want to be.

Objective:

Students will be able to create an Internet meme based off research that promotes the Condition of Belonging.

Materials:

Internet, device or computer, photo-editing software or app, for example, Meme Something. Modify to use markers and posters, if technology not available.

Steps:

Instruct students to research ways to increase Belonging, respect, or tolerance in middle schools or middle school classrooms. Based on their research, have students pick a topic related to Belonging on which to focus. For example, students can research the effectiveness of mix-it-up lunch days or anti-bullying strategies.

Students should then apply their knowledge to create an Internet meme that supports their topic.

- Students should analyze popular Internet memes and look for patterns. What characteristics do they share? Students should create a meme with their audience in mind.

- Students should decide who their audience is. Is it teachers? Principals? Their classmates? Younger students? Students of all ages?

- Next, students can brainstorm ideas for their new meme. Students will pick the visual for their meme by searching the Web, taking their own original photographs, creating an original graphic design, or drawing a picture. Students can also come up with creative tag lines that will catch their audiences' attention.

- Using your meme app of choice, have students select a photo from their gallery or take a new photograph. Then write a creative text line.
- Next, have students decide what information they want to go along with the meme when they post it online. They may consider posting a question, a relevant quote, a surprising statistic, or Web links to informative resource pages. Check out the Student Voice National Report for some relevant information (www.qisa.org).
- Have students upload and share their meme on their own social networks and other online communities.

Source: Photo by Julie Hellerstein.

Personal Reflection:

- What did you learn from this assignment?
- How much awareness were you able to generate?
- What kind of feedback did you receive from peers or your target audience?

Group Discussion:

Have students share their post with the class and explain their related relevant research. Invite other students to ask relevant questions about their purpose, research, and meme.

Extended Learning:

Have students track the retweets, regrams, or likes on their memes. Use a free trial of social media sites like sproutsocial.com or hootsuite.com. What content received the most feedback? What kind of feedback did it receive?

Notes:

_____

_____

_____

_____

_____

CHAPTER 2

Heroes

Each semester to make sure every student knows that staff care about them as more than just students, one school prints out and puts their entire co-curricular calendar on a wall in the staff room. Sporting events are listed and so are practices; theatrical and band performances are listed and also rehearsals. In all, there are approximately 300 time blocks. At the start of each semester, the staff are asked to put their initials in at least three boxes so that the entire co-curricular schedule is covered. This creates an experience for both students and staff of feeling respected and valued beyond the classroom and hallways. In this school, no student doubts that adults care.

Having a Hero—a role model, mentor, teacher, or any trusted other—is critical to a student's success at school. Numerous studies point out the importance of such positive relationships to students' academic, social, and personal well-being. Students tell us all the time that they work harder for teachers they believe care about and respect them and will actually withhold work from teachers they believe do not.

Once younger students are over the idea that Batman and Wonder Woman are Heroes, and once older students are over the idea that Tom Brady and Serena Williams are Heroes, they share that the everyday Heroes in their lives, the people that make a difference are their parents, their teachers, their friends, and people in the community like police officers and firefighters. While it may make some educators uncomfortable to be thought of as Heroes, this is what students say. There is no escaping the fact that second only to parents, teachers are among the most influential people any of us encounter in the course of a lifetime. Check this against your own experience: Consider the number of teachers that have had an influence on your life.

The characteristics that young people identify in the people they consider Heroes are obvious ones like attention, respect, concern, and care. But there are also less obvious ones like having high expectations and holding them accountable for their actions and schoolwork. It is not just the "nice" teachers that are accounted Heroes by students, but the ones who will not let them get away with things, who "call us on our stuff," and who make clear what the boundaries and expectations are.

In addition to the adults in a school being Heroes to students, students can be Heroes to one another. Whether a student finds care and kindness among her peer group and friends, or whether older students encourage and mentor younger students, all students can learn to play this supportive role for one another. The following activites will guide you to help students recognize the everyday Heroes among them and help you teach them how to be Heroes to one another.

Breaking News

(ABOUT 50 MINUTES)

Heroes:

Having people who believe in you and are there for you when you need them.

Objective:

Students will be able to identify characteristics that every day Heroes or role models possess. Students will be able to use relevant details and information to convey the essence of their Hero.

Materials:

Classroom set of devices (iPads, iPods, or iPhones); TouchCast app; access to newspapers, online articles, or other media for current events.

Steps:

- Tell students they are going to identify everyday Hero characteristics. The class will work together to compile a list of traits.

- Have students look for stories in the local news and media about everyday people being Heroes. What characteristics do these people possess?

- Next, have students create an essay about someone who is their Hero. Students should be very descriptive and provide telling details to portray a vivid picture. Essays should include the following information:

  o Who is an influential person or role model or Hero in your life?

  o What do you admire about this Hero?

  o What specific things has this person taught you or which specific areas of your life have they impacted?

- How have you used what your role model taught you in your daily life?
- A quote from this person that reflects their character.
- A quick story or anecdote about this person.

- Have students create a real looking news report using the TouchCast app to present the information from their essay. Students can pick a theme for their news background, such as sports, classic news report, or Instacast. Students should upload a Twitter feed or Google news report on Heroes or a topic related to their report to have in the background of their news report. Students can also upload pictures of their Hero, graphs, quotes, and create textboxes to emphasize their main points. Students can also select a green screen feature to change the background and also select a filter to convey a theme or upload their own music and sound effects.

Source: Created using TouchCast.

Personal Reflection:

- How did this activity impact your understanding of everyday Heroes?
- Why is it important to give special recognition to your everyday Hero?
- When have you acted like an everyday Hero?

Group Reflection:

Have students share their presentations. After the presentations, students should identify similarities and differences among the characteristics of the Heroes. How do you see students being everyday Heroes?

Extended Learning:

Create a YouTube Class Heroes channel. Upload students' videos to the channel. Next, have students' research and identify other relevant video clips about characteristics of every day Heroes, current events in the news about Heroes, or more information on their Heroes. Add these videos to the channel, too. Have students share their work and the class's ideas with peers, parents, and community members. Students can also write and post discussion questions on videos to spark an interesting conversation.

Heroes Here in the Classroom

(FIRST DAY: 30 MINUTES; PERSONAL AND
GROUP REFLECTION: 20 MINUTES)

Common Core:
CCSS.ELA-LITERACY.W.9-10.6
Use technology, including the Internet, to produce, publish, and update individual or shared writing products, taking advantage of technology's capacity to link to other information and to display information flexibly and dynamically.

21st Century Skills:
Critical Thinking and Problem Solving, Creativity and Innovation, Communication, Collaboration, ICT Literacy, Media Literacy

ISTE/NETS:
Creativity and innovation B

Communication and collaboration A

Digital citizenship B

Technology operations and concepts A, B

Heroes:

Having people who believe in you and are there for you when you need them.

Objective:

Students will be able to recognize that they are Heroes to the people they interact with every day. Students will be able to identify ways that they can be an everyday Hero at school and in the community.

Materials:

List of student actions to post online, on board, or in handouts for students.

Steps:

- Review the list of student actions on the Condition of Heroes by putting the list on the board or creating a shared Google document.
  - ○ Volunteer to work with someone on a group project who is often left out.
- ○ Speak out when you see someone being treated unfairly
- ○ Take the time to thank the school custodians, lunch workers, and secretaries.
- ○ Mentor or give advice to a new student.
- ○ Mentor or give advice to a younger student.
- ○ Seek out an adult at school you can talk to about issues. Introduce yourself and check in with this person on a regular basis.
- ○ Actively respect students who are different from you.
- ○ Write a letter or create a social media post to thank someone who has been a Hero to you.

- Tweet a picture of your Hero and explain what characteristics and personal traits you admire. Challenge your peers to do the same.
- Post a quote about everyday Heroes to Instagram. Write a caption explaining the importance of Heroes. Challenge your peers to do the same.
- Watch a movie or TV show that relates to the Condition of Heroes. Explain to your class what you learned from it and how it could apply to your school.
- Identify a short story that relates to the Condition of Heroes. Explain what you learned to your class.
- Identify informational text or a nonfiction piece that relates to the Condition of Heroes. Explain what you learned to your class.
- Find and post lyrics to a song that reminds you of the Condition of Heroes.
- Invite your teachers to eat lunch with you and your friends.
- Using an app like Red Stamp, create, and send a personalized thank you note to a peer.
- Watch *Two Young Heroes: Danny and Tommy* at http://ellentube.com/videos/0-11fwrim2/ with your fellow students write about and discuss what it means to be a Hero.
- Nominate your Hero at the Foundation for a Better Life site at http://www.values.com/.
- Send letters of thanks and support to soldiers (home and abroad), law enforcement officers, EMTs, firefighters, or nurses.
- Interview your principal about the importance of Heroes and share what you learned with the team.
- Write a thank you note to a Hero using Punchbowl free, digital thank-you cards.

- As you review the list, invite students to create other ideas on how they can be Heroes.
- Have students sign up for the Heroes task of their choice.
- Create a class list to hold students accountable for their actions.
- Students will document or record their evidence of their action through video recording, audio recording, pictures, or journal reflection.

Personal Reflection:

- How did your action help foster the Condition of Heroes?
- How do you see yourself being a Hero every day?
- How do you see your classmates being Heroes every day?

Group Reflection:

Students can present their findings in small groups. Students should discuss the following questions and create a shared writing product via Google docs, class blog, or traditional journals.

Gratitude

(20–30 MINUTES)

Heroes:

Having people who believe in you and are there for you when you need them. Often when students think of Heroes, they talk about famous athletes or celebrities. However, there are everyday people who make a difference in our lives by talking to us and listening to us.

Objective:

Students will be able to recognize the everyday Heroes in their lives. Students will be able to produce clear and coherent writing to thank a Hero.

Materials:

Thank-you cards or computers with access to http://www.punch bowl.com/ecards/thank-you?gclid=CJjxg7KpncECFYMF7A odu3oALg.

> **Common Core:**
> CCSS.ELA-LITERACY.CCRA.W.4 Produce clear and coherent writing in which the development, organization, and style are appropriate to task, purpose, and audience.
>
> CCSS.ELA-LITERACY.CCRA.W.6 Use technology, including the Internet, to produce and publish writing and to interact and collaborate with others.
>
> **21st Century Skills:**
> Communication and Collaboration, Leadership and Responsibility
>
> **ISTE/NETS:**
> Creativity and innovation B
> Digital citizenship D

Steps:

- Ask students to think of a teacher, coach, neighbor or staff member who really believes in them.
- Allow students to share stories or anecdotes.
- Next, instruct students to write a thank-you note or card of appreciation to a person who made a difference in their life. Students can create a handwritten card or a free, digital card using punchbowl.com.
- For the digital card, have students Google punch bowl free thank you notes and select a template. Students will edit and design the front, inside, and the envelope and postage to send to their Hero.
- Students should give specific reasons and identify the characteristics of the person that makes them their Hero.
- Once the cards are complete, encourage students to send the card.

Personal Reflection:

- Who is your most important everyday Hero right now? Explain.
- Who do you think you are a Hero to and why?

Group Reflection:

Besides writing thank-you cards, what else could we do to show our gratitude to people who are everyday Heroes to us? Make a list on the board of creative ways to say thank you.

Next, brainstorm ways to build relationships and get to know other staff members or adults in your life.

- Interview your principal.
- Invite a teacher to eat lunch with you and your friends.
- Pick out one adult at school you would like to get to know better and talk to them once a week during your free time.
- Take the time to get to know the school custodians, lunch workers, secretaries, and other support staff.

Extended Learning:

Share your gratitude 2.0!

- Create an iMovie trailer using superhero format to recognize a role model. Focus on the characteristics you admire about this role model.
- Nominate your Hero at the Foundation for a Better Life site at http://www.values .com/.
- Using an app such as Red Stamp, create and send a personalized thank-you note to your everyday Hero.
- Tweet about your Hero!
- Create an Instagram post about your Hero. Select a picture of you and your Hero, a quote that reminds you of your Hero, or even a selfie of your Hero. Explain why this person makes a difference to you!
- Create a YouTube video about your Hero!
- If your teacher has a website or a class blog, ask if you can post your writing there! Blogger is an easy blog tool.

CHAPTER 3

Sense of Accomplishment

Traditional report cards draw students' (and parents') eyes toward the letter or number grade that represents a summation of scores given for attendance, assignments, home-work, quizzes, tests, and exams. This summation inevitably hides information critical to the learning process. For example, a student who starts with zeros and ends with hun-dreds would have a GPA of 2.0 as would a student who started with hundreds and ended with zeros. Yet clearly these students have taken different paths and ended up in differ-ent places. That's why one school redesigned its report card to include a prominent place for effort and student self-assessment in each subject area. Together with tradi-tional grading this creates a much more accurate summary of what students are capable of at any single point in time.

Consider how often you or your school recognizes and celebrates a student's achievement—that is to say: *what* they produce. Most schools do a good job of holding honor roll assemblies to reward academic achievement and awards banquets to reward athletic achievement. Some schools even have art fairs, where those who produce excellent works of art are recognized anpd noted with ribbons. This is important and should continue. In addition, schools should also be places that recognize and celebrate effort, perseverance, good citizenship and all the many talents and gifts that students possess. A Sense of Accomplishment comes not just from having crossed the finish line first but from the effort put into running the race well.

First of all, effort and perseverance count for more toward the attainment of a person's aspirations than achievement. Getting all As may be easy for some students, whereas getting a solid C through hard work and study may be a challenge for others. Scoring touchdowns may be second nature to a young man who hit the genetic lottery, while just making the team requires hours of working out and preparation for another. It turns out that in life, this latter set of characteristics—those currently associated with *grit*—is more associated with success than the end product that typically gets so much attention in school.

Secondly, being a good citizen of the school is touted as important in mission statements and by administrators, yet how often are kindness and thoughtfulness applauded and upheld? It is easy to pay lip service to the behavioral ideals expressed in values statements and codes of conduct, but rarely are those who go out of their way to help and support others given the same recognition as those who excel academically or athletically.

Thirdly, while our students are multitalented, the set of talents celebrated in schools is fairly narrow. Frequently those who are exceptional in the classroom or on the field have recognition assemblies, while those with as exceptional talent in music or theater or dance or comedy or photography or interpersonal relationships or preparing food or skateboarding or . . . you get the idea—look on from the audience.

The following exercises will help you and your students see beyond what they achieve as a hallmark of success and look at the effort and perseverance that go into being successful. The exercises also help students expand the categories of what counts for accomplishment. Together you will learn that, although the primary purpose of school involves academics, academics need not be the only category in which we celebrate one another.

Scholarship

(40–50 MINUTES)

Sense of Accomplishment:

Being recognized for many different types of success, including hard work and being a good person. Sense of Accomplishment is about all your talents and skills rather than just skills that are measured by tests and grades.

Objective:

Students will be able to evaluate and compare different types of success.

Materials:

New York Times articles; paper and pencil or device.

Steps:

- Read two articles from the *New York Times*.

    1. "What Criteria Should Be Used in Awarding Scholarships for College?" *at* http://learning.blogs.nytimes.com/2013/09/09/what-criteria-should-be-used-in-awarding-scholarships-for-college/?_r=0.

    2. "Tuition Aid From a Zombie Elf" at http://www.nytimes.com/2013/09/08/nyregion/tuition-aid-from-a-zombie-elf.html?_r=0.

- Answer comprehension questions below and then the reaction questions listed at the bottom of the first article. Have students write out responses.

    ○ What is the author's point of view? What rhetoric does the author use to support his or her point of view?

    ○ How effective was the author's argument? What points make the author's position clear, convincing, and engaging? What points were not engaging to you?

    ○ What do you think are the best indicators that a student deserves a scholarship? Why? How does this compare to the author's point of view?

> **Common Core:**
> CCSS.ELA-LITERACY.RI.9-10.6 Determine an author's point of view or purpose in a text and analyze how an author uses rhetoric to advance that point of view or purpose.
>
> CCSS.ELA-LITERACY.RI.11-12.5 Analyze and evaluate the effectiveness of the structure an author uses in his or her exposition or argument, including whether the structure makes points clear, convincing, and engaging.
>
> **21st Century Skills:**
> Creativity and Innovation, Critical Thinking and Problem Solving
>
> **ISTE/NETS:**
> Creativity and innovation B
> Research and information fluency B
> Critical thinking D

- How does the experience of someone who is extremely involved with an interest such as the trading card game, Magic: The Gathering, compare to those of another student who is more engaged with school-run extracurricular activities?
- What other nonschool activities might be worth considering as a basis for awarding a scholarship? Why?

- Create a unique pretend scholarship: Identify a skill or unique talent that you are proud of. Next, create a scholarship for your talent. Give your scholarship a name, describe what the scholarship stands for or represents, the amount of money being offered, and what qualifications applicants should have. Next, create an essay question that your applicants will answer.
- Have students present their scholarship.

Personal Reflection:

What skills and outlooks have you gained from after-school activities, both school-related and otherwise, that you have chosen to pursue?

Group Reflection:

- Why is it important to recognize a variety of talents and accomplishments? Besides scholarships, how else are students' accomplishments formally recognized?

Extended Learning:

Encourage students to research available scholarship awards based on their aspirations or goals for the future. Give them time to write their essays or create a video for the scholarship, based on the requirements.

Notes:

_____

_____

_____

_____

_____

_____

What About the Rest of the Alphabet?

(ABOUT 30 MINUTES)

Sense of Accomplishment:

Sense of Accomplishment is about recognizing all kinds of accomplishments. In schools, students who earn As and Bs on their report cards are honored academically and students who wear letters on their jackets are recognized for their athletic accomplishments. Without taking anything away from those successes, how can we expand on what we celebrate and reward at school?

Objective:

Students will be able to identify ways to rate and reward accomplishments other than academic and athletic success. Students will be able to think critically about how to broaden what we value in schools.

Materials:

Papers, pens, and pencils; Google document (optional).

Steps:

- Use these questions to begin this activity:
  - What things do we celebrate and recognize as accomplishments in our school?
  - What is one thing you would like to achieve this school year?
- Ask your students to consider accomplishments they have attained that are not athletic or academic. Encourage students to think of all sorts of accomplishments, such as making a new friend, getting a job, or passing a driving test.
- Post students' accomplishments on the board. Have students write their accomplishments on a Google document or have students take turns writing down their accomplishments on a whiteboard.
- In pairs, have students pick four different accomplishments from the board. Have students create a new grading scale for each of the four accomplishments. The grading scale must

> **Common Core:**
> CCSS.ELA-LITERACY.SL.9-10.1
> Initiate and participate effectively in a range of collaborative discussions (one-on-one, in groups, and teacher-led) with diverse partners on grades 9-10 topics, texts, and issues, building on others' ideas and expressing their own clearly and persuasively.
>
> **21st Century Skills:**
> Critical Thinking and Problem Solving, Creativity and Innovation
>
> **ISTE/NETS:**
> Creativity and innovation B

use four consecutive letters of the alphabet to rate achievements. For example, for passing a driving test the scale might be G = Great driver, H = Hide if you see me coming, I = Stay indoors if I am on the road, J = Jail.

- Encourage students to create a visual aid that contains the grading scale with a picture using Red Stamp app, PicCollage, or another app. Have students share their clever grading systems.

Personal Reflection:

What accomplishments should receive greater recognition in school? What impact would this have on students? Write a persuasive essay.

Source: Photo by Julie Hellerstein.

Group Reflection:

- Why do schools limit themselves to recognizing mostly academic and athletic accomplishments?
- How can we celebrate the items on the board for the remainder of the year?

Extended Learning:

In the group reflection, students discussed how to celebrate the items on the board for the remainder of the year. Based on the discussion, partner with students to design and implement a new student recognition system.

Here are some examples:

- Create a Twitter account that mentions students for their hard work and being good citizens.
- Create a Hall of Fame board where students can post their accomplishments, hang artwork and assignments they are proud of.
- Award students tickets for participation. Tickets can be redeemed for a homework pass or another incentive.
- Create a Class Dojo system. Show students' video on class dojo at http://teach2.class dojo.com/#!/launchpad. Use this tool that tracks students' accomplishments like participation, helping others, persistence, teamwork, helping others and staying on task. Teacher will grant students dojo points. At the end of the day, students will find out how they have done and what they can improve. Students all get to create their own avatar too!

Snapshot Show and Tell

(30–40 MINUTES)

Sense of Accomplishment:

Sense of Accomplishment is about celebrating the importance of effort and perseverance as signs of your success. The Condition is about trying repeatedly and facing challenges rather than giving up. Sense of Accomplishment is about all your talents and skill rather than just skills that are measured by tests and grades.

Objective:

Students will be able to create a narrative to illustrate an accomplishment they have attained that required effort and perseverance.

Materials:

Pen and paper or device; photographs; students' personal phones or devices.

Steps:

- Ask students to select an accomplishment that they are proud of that required effort and perseverance. Students should explain what their motivation was to keep going and the outcome of their perseverance and how they felt about their accomplishment.

- Students should then write a narrative using effective technique, well-chosen details, and well-structured event sequences to describe their accomplishment.

- Invite students to share their narrative in a show and tell format. Students should also bring in a snapshot or original picture that helps illustrate their narrative.

- Students should sit in a circle and share and pass their picture around or have it projected on screen for all students to see.

Common Core:
CCSS.ELA-LITERACY.W.9-10.3
Write narratives to develop real or imagined experiences or events using effective technique, well-chosen details, and well-structured event sequences.

CCSS.ELA-LITERACY.W.9-10.3.B
Use narrative techniques, such as dialogue, pacing, description, reflection, and multiple plot lines, to develop experiences, events, and/or characters.

CCSS.ELA-LITERACY.W.9-10.3.C
Use a variety of techniques to sequence events so that they build on one another to create a coherent whole.

CCSS.ELA-LITERACY.W.9-10.3.D
Use precise words and phrases, telling details, and sensory language to convey a vivid picture of the experiences, events, setting, and/or characters.

21st Century Skills:
Communication, Creativity and Innovation

ISTE/NETS:
Creativity and innovation B
Communication and collaboration B

Personal Reflection:

Have students score themselves for each of the following statements using the scale: Always = 4, Most of the time = 3, Sometimes = 2, Rarely = 1, Never = 0.

1. I put forth effort even if an assignment is not graded.

2. I am willing to redo assignments to improve my work.

3. I put forth effort to be a good citizen.

4. I make sure my peers know they can count on me to try my best.

5. I am proud of my accomplishments.

6. I seek help when I struggle academically.

7. I participate in class discussions.

8. I try my best on assignments and tests.

Have students choose two of their lower responses and consider what it would take to get them to answer "Always" next time.

Group Reflection:

- Why do some people seem to give up more quickly than others?
- How can students motivate themselves to put forth 100% effort?
- Does having a goal in mind help a person persevere?
- What kind of attitude do you need to persevere in hard situations?

Extended Learning:

Watch this commercial, *Duracell: Trust Your Power NFL Derrick Coleman, Seattle Seahawks,* at http://www.usatoday.com/videos/news/2014/12/13/20352837/. Create your own commercial using your narrative focusing on perseverance. Be sure to pick a product of your choice.

Notes:

_____

_____

_____

Marble Roll

(ABOUT 30 MINUTES)

Sense of Accomplishment:

Sense of Accomplishment is about celebrating the importance of effort and perseverance as signs of your success. The Condition is about trying repeatedly and facing challenges rather than giving up. Sense of Accomplishment is about all your talents and skill rather than just skills that are measured by tests and grades.

Objective:

Students will be able to discuss the importance of effort and perseverance. Students will be able to reflect on what is valued in school.

Materials:

Half a paper towel roll cut lengthwise for every student; four or five marbles; *Famous Failures* YouTube video; Edmodo (for extended learning).

> **Common Core:**
> CCSS.ELA-LITERACY.SL.9-10.1 Initiate and participate effectively in a range of collaborative discussions (one-on-one, in groups, and teacher-led) with diverse partners on grades 9-10 topics, texts, and issues, building on others' ideas and expressing their own clearly and persuasively.
>
> **21st Century Skills:**
> Communication and Collaboration
>
> **ISTE/NETS:**
> Communication and collaboration D

Steps:

- Divide students into teams of five to seven. Give each student a half tube and have teams stand at one end of the room.

- Establish a starting point (A) and an ending point (B). The distance can be about the length of a standard classroom.

- Tell students that the challenge is to move the marble from one end of the room to the other using the half paper tube. Have students line up and start the marble by rolling it down the half tube toward his or her teammate. The next person on the team catches the marble in his or her tube and proceeds to roll it and drop it into the next person's tube. Continue doing this until the team reaches point B. Students cannot carry the marble in their tube.

- Tell teams they will receive a grade for this activity. However, do not tell them what you are grading. Instead of a traditional grade that rewards the team who came in first with an A, second B, and so on, distribute grades based on teamwork, effort, perseverance or having the most fun.

- Follow up with the YouTube video *Famous Failures*. Ask: What did these famous people do after they experienced failure? Lead a discussion about the importance of effort and perseverance. How do these characteristics affect schoolwork? What does effort and perseverance look like in school?

Personal Reflection:

Reflect on a time that you wanted to give up because an assignment or task was too hard.

- What strategies did you use to overcome this frustration?
- Why did you put forth effort on this project?
- What was the outcome?

Group Reflection:

- Were you surprised by your groups' grade in the marble activity? Why or why not?
- What accomplishments are typically recognized in schools? In addition to those accomplishments, what other types of accomplishments should be recognized?
- Why are effort and hard work important?

Extended Learning:

Based on the *Famous Failures* video, students can identify and research a person who has illustrated great perseverance and effort. Students should write a brief report on what motivated the person, how the person persevered or showed effort, and what the outcome was. Students can share their report on Edmodo or a social media network of their choice.

Notes:

_____

_____

_____

_____

_____

_____

_____

Student Actions

(INITIAL ACTIVITY: 20–30 MINUTES; FOLLOW-UP
A FEW DAYS LATER: 20–30 MINUTES)

Sense of Accomplishment:

Sense of Accomplishment is about celebrating the importance of effort and perseverance as signs of your success. The Condition is about trying repeatedly and facing challenges rather than giving up. Sense of Accomplishment is about all your talents and skill rather than just skills that are measured by tests and grades.

Objective:

Students will be able to execute an action step or plan to improve their Sense of Accomplishment.

Materials:

List of student actions related to Sense of Accomplishment to post online, on board, or handouts for students.

Steps:

- Start with a discussion about Sense of Accomplishment: What does it feel like to persevere? How do you see students putting forth effort at school? Why do you think it is important for students to be good citizens? What could you do today to be a better citizen at school or in your community? What can you do to develop the Condition of Sense of Accomplishment for yourself?

- Tell students that they will take action to develop the Condition of Sense of Accomplishment. Post and review the following list of student actions on the board or create a shared Google document.

  o Revise an assignment just to improve your own understanding.

  o Tutor a peer or friend who is struggling in a certain subject.

  o If you are not an avid reader, read a book of your choice just for yourself.

  o Make a to-do list every day for one week. To what extent did you reach your goals?

Common Core:
CCSS.ELA-LITERACY.SL.9-10.1
Initiate and participate effectively in a range of collaborative discussions (one-on-one, in groups, and teacher-led) with diverse partners on grades 9-10 topics, texts, and issues, building on others' ideas and expressing their own clearly and persuasively.
CCSS.ELA-LITERACY.W.9-10.4
Produce clear and coherent writing in which the development, organization, and style are appropriate to task, purpose, and audience.

21st Century Skills:
Collaboration, Initiative and Self-Direction, Leadership and Responsibility

ISTE/NETS:
Communication and collaboration B, D

- Set a physical goal for yourself like running a 5k race. Log your training and preparation. Reflect on the experience. How did you feel a Sense of Accomplishment?
- Organize your school folders, notebooks, binders, or device.
- Solve a difficult Sudoku puzzle.
- When a task seems overwhelming, don't give up.
- Ask a teacher for suggestions and feedback beyond a letter grade.
- Get a new high score on a game.
- Solve a difficult math problem.
- Create a social media post of something you are proud of!
- Watch a movie or TV show where the character experiences a Sense of Accomplishment because of his or her perseverance, hard work, or citizenship.
- Create a Sense of Accomplishment poster or bulletin board with quotes, pictures, or a list of related traits. Be sure to get permission from teacher or school staff.
- Write a goal and put it in your shoe. When you accomplish it, rip it up and write a new one.
- Figure out how to knit or learn another hands-on craft.
- Finish something that you started a while ago but never got to.
- Hang up your schoolwork on your refrigerator, in your locker, or in your room. Make sure it is work where you improved or gave good effort!
- Write in your planner one thing that you are proud of every day for one month.

Source: Photo by Julie Hellerstein.

- Create a list of what you accomplished this year, this month, this week, and today.
  - Work ahead on a long-term project for school.
  - Clean your room. Take a before and after picture and compare.
  - Participate in a community service activity.
- As you review the list, invite students to create other ideas on how they can have a Sense of Accomplishment.
- Have students sign up for the Sense of Accomplishment task of their choice. You may decide more than one student can do a task.
- Create a class list to hold students accountable to their action.
- Students should document or record their evidence of their action through video recording, audio recording, pictures, or journal reflection.
- Debrief the purpose of the activity and establish a due date.

Personal Reflection:

How did your action help foster the Condition of Sense of Accomplishment?

Group Reflection:

Students should share what they learned from undertaking the above actions in a large group. Then, break students into small groups. Have students read and discuss the statements below to guide a discussion or debate. Students should pay attention whether their peers have different ideas about each statement.

- Effort is just as important as getting good grades.
- Adults only care about good grades.
- Tests are not the only way to see if I know something.
- Good grades are most important factor for college.
- It is important to be involved with community service.
- Trying harder doesn't mean I will do better.
- Some students get good grades even though they put forth little effort.

Extended Learning:

Create a whole-school challenge for every student to take an action step that fosters the Condition of Sense of Accomplishment. Find an effective way to communicate challenges with the rest of the student body.

- Create a Twitter account that posts different Sense of Accomplishment challenges.
- Ask the school website to post the list or pass out action cards at lunch.
- Create a bulletin board inviting students to try actions.

Revise an assignment just to improve your own understanding.	Tutor a peer or friend who is struggling in a certain subject.	Clean your room or organize your locker. Take a before and after picture and compare.	Make a to-do list every day for one week. To what extent did you reach your goals?
Set a physical goal for yourself like running a 5k race. Log your training and preparation. Reflect on the experience. How did you feel a Sense of Accomplishment?	Organize your school folders, notebooks, binders, or device.	Solve a difficult Sudoku puzzle.	When a task seems overwhelming, don't give up.
Ask a teacher for suggestions and feedback beyond a letter grade.	Get a new high score on a game.	Solve a difficult math problem.	Create a social media post of something you are proud of!
Watch a movie or TV show where the character experiences a Sense of Accomplishment because of his or her perseverance, hard work, or citizenship.	Create a Sense of Accomplishment poster or bulletin board with quotes, pictures, or a list of related traits. Be sure to get permission from teacher or school staff.	Write a goal and put it in your shoe. When you accomplish it, rip it up and write a new one.	Figure out how to knit or learn another hands-on craft.
Finish something that you started a while ago but never got to.	Hang up your schoolwork on your refrigerator, in your locker, or in your room. Make sure it is work where you improved or gave good effort!	Write in your planner one thing that you are proud of every day for one month.	Create a list of what you accomplished this year, this month, this week, and today.

Headline News

(ABOUT 50 MINUTES)

Sense of Accomplishment:

Sense of Accomplishment is about recognizing all the things students do that are accomplishments. Students should be proud of their accomplishments whether they are big or small. This activity encourages students to realize that accomplishments can be more than good grades and sports trophies.

Objective:

Students will be able to plan, write, and format a digital newspaper article about their accomplishments in a clear and coherent manner.

Materials:

Computers or devices with newspaper template of your choice. Free template is available at http://www.readwritethink.org/files/resources/interactives/Printing_Press/. Free templates also available on Google docs.

Steps:

In this activity, students will write a front page for their own newspaper that highlights their accomplishments. Students have all kinds of accomplishments like being a good citizen, working hard, persevering, not giving up on a difficult task.

- Warm-up activity: Students will answer the following questions: What have you accomplished this school year? This month? This week? What accomplishments have you been recognized for in school or in the community? What is something you want to accomplish this year?

- Explain to students that they will be creating a newspaper that highlights their accomplishments. Bring in newspapers for students to view. Students can also review newspaper articles online. Students will select a front-page story and describe what makes it interesting.

Common Core:
CCSS.ELA-LITERACY.W.6.2
Write informative/explanatory texts to examine a topic and convey ideas, concepts, and information through the selection, organization, and analysis of relevant content.

CCSS.ELA-LITERACY.W.6.2.A
Introduce a topic; organize ideas, concepts, and information, using strategies such as definition, classification, comparison/contrast, and cause/effect; include formatting (e.g., headings), graphics (e.g., charts, tables), and multimedia when useful to aiding comprehension.

CCSS.ELA-LITERACY.W.6.2.B
Develop the topic with relevant facts, definitions, concrete details, quotations, or other information and examples.

CCSS.ELA-LITERACY.W.6.2.C
Use appropriate transitions to clarify the relationships among ideas and concepts.

CCSS.ELA-LITERACY.W.6.2.D
Use precise language and domain-specific vocabulary to inform about or explain the topic.

CCSS.ELA-LITERACY.W.6.4
Produce clear and coherent writing in which the development, organization, and style are appropriate to task, purpose, and audience.

CCSS.ELA-LITERACY.W.6.5
With some guidance and support from peers and adults, develop and strengthen writing as needed by planning, revising, editing, rewriting, or trying a new approach.

CCSS.ELA-LITERACY.W.6.6
Use technology, including the Internet, to produce and publish writing as well as to interact and collaborate with others; demonstrate sufficient command of keyboarding skills to type a minimum of three pages in a single sitting.

21st Century Skills:
Media Literacy, Critical Thinking Skills, Communication, Creativity and Innovation

ISTE/NETS:
Creativity and innovation B
Communication and collaboration B

- Discuss as a class: What makes a front-page story interesting? What strategies do effective journalists use?

- Students will develop a newspaper name, one headline article, and several shorter articles that illustrate their accomplishments. Students should include details, facts, and what kind of effort, traits, and skills were required.

- Students may use their warm-up activity as a starting point. Allow students time to think, plan, and create their front pages.

- Students will use a word document newspaper template or other newspaper template to create a newspaper rough draft.

- With a partner, students should peer edit and give feedback.

- Encourage students to upload pictures that illustrate their stories.

- Hot off the presses! Post students' articles in your classroom or post on class website. If students' headline articles are in pdf, upload into youblisher.com to turn into a publication with flipping pages.

Personal Reflection:

- Why is it important to feel recognized for a variety of achievements?
- What is the best way for peers, teachers, friends, and family to recognize you for these accomplishments?

Group Reflection:

Celebrating each other's headlines is a great way to acknowledge the accomplishments of our peers. How can we continue to celebrate all of our accomplishments?

Extended Learning:

Brainstorm, create and implement a class procedure or system that routinely celebrates students for a variety of accomplishments.

Here are some ideas to get you started:

- Watch the video clip from *Legally Blonde 2, Snap Cup Builds Group Cohesion*. Design your own snap cup. Students will recognize peers accomplishments by writing down their achievements. Once a week, read the slips of paper aloud and have everyone snap along as a way to applaud each other.

- Create a class Twitter account that mentions students for their hard work and being good citizens. Students can Tweet about their peers and give them shout outs.

- Create a Hall of Fame board where students can post their accomplishments, hang artwork, and share assignments they are proud of.
- Award students tickets for participation. Tickets can be redeemed for a homework pass or other incentive.
- Create a Class Dojo system. Show the students a video on class dojo at http://teach2 .classdojo.com/#!/launchpad. Visit this tool that tracks students' accomplishments like participation, helping others, persistence, teamwork, helping others and staying on task. You can grant students dojo points. At the end of the day, students will find out how they have done and what they can improve. Students all get to create their own avatar too.

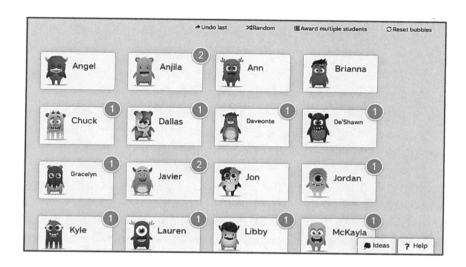

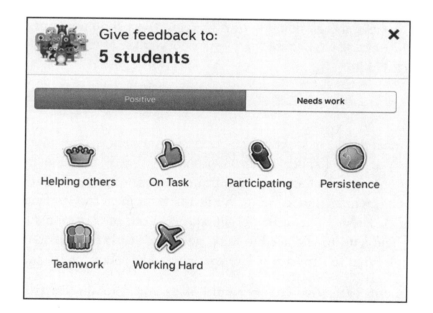

Source: Courtesy of Class Dojo.

CHAPTER 4

Fun & Excitement

Teaching is fun. That was our experience and it is what teachers tell us all the time when we visit schools. Developing a lesson plan, helping other people learn, seeing the light bulb go off over someone's head because you flipped the right switch is engaging, exciting, and emotionally fulfilling. That's why at one high school teaching is an activity shared by adults and young people. Students regularly co-teach with their teachers. Far beyond student presentations as part of an assessment rubric, each week time is set aside for a team of students and teachers to look ahead to upcoming content that must be learned and mastered and work together to come up with lesson plans, strategies, activities, learning experiences, and assessments. Students are adept, connecting content to pop culture and music, and regularly find creative ways to make material understandable to their peers. Adults bring their greater experience to structuring time, using tried and true tactics, and avoiding known pitfalls. Over the course of the year, every student participates on the teaching team every six weeks. At this school, learning is fun because teaching is fun.

We sometimes meet people in schools who believe seriousness and fun are mutually exclusive—that learning can only happen in an environment that is emotionally sterile. This runs counter to our experience and, by the way, a significant amount of research that makes a connection between emotional engagement and learning. While many teachers and students believe that learning can be fun, Fun & Excitement seems to get squeezed out of classrooms by rigid curriculum, strict pacing guides, and a do-or-die need to make adequate yearly progress (AYP). Fun, if it exists at all in schools, is relegated to extracurricular experiences like sports, clubs, and field trips.

Yet Fun & Excitement—affective engagement—is essential to sustain the focus and energy required to learn something deeply and well. Consider how difficult it is to learn material you find boring or to pay attention to someone who is dull no matter how important what they are saying is. The fact of the matter is our students are each a "whole child." That is to say, they come to us not just with an intellect, but also with emotions. Not just with thoughts, but with feelings. Not just with a mind, but also with a body that, during the school years, is growing and energetic and needs to move far more often than most children have a chance to when they are at school. We ourselves are better teachers when we reveal the passion we have for a particular subject or for learning itself. Students tell us all the time about how much they enjoy a class because of the obvious love of the subject matter the teacher has.

Creating a learning environment that is emotionally engaging is not about the teacher finding ways to entertain the students. Educators would have a hard time competing with the resources available to the entertainment industry. Nor, as with the other Conditions, is Fun & Excitement solely the teacher's responsibility. Students are responsible for behavior that can allow for fun without becoming chaotic, as well as for being in touch with their interests and passions as it connects to what is being studied. Together teachers and students can create classroom experiences that are both educational and enjoyable.

Fun & Excitement as a Condition that supports student aspirations is not about telling jokes or taking a break from studies to do something amusing that does not involve learning. Fun & Excitement is about ensuring the learning we are doing is engaging, that we are passionate about what we are studying, and that we connect to it on an emotional level. When Fun & Excitement is present in a classroom environment, time passes quickly as everyone becomes immersed in the learning experience. While not every lesson in every subject can be utterly engrossing every day, the following exercises will help you and your students discover the Fun & Excitement that is available to you while learning. Together you will explore how technology, social experiences, everyday relevance, and physical movement can reverse the boredom that might accompany otherwise traditionally dull experiences in school.

Tweet Teach

(30–50 MINUTES)

Common Core:
CCSS.ELA-LITERACY.W.9-10.4
Produce clear and coherent writing in which the development, organization, and style are appropriate to task, purpose, and audience

CCSS.ELA-LITERACY.W.9-10.6
Use technology, including the Internet, to produce, publish, and update individual or shared writing products, taking advantage of technology's capacity to link to other information and to display information flexibly and dynamically.

21st Century Skills:
Communication, Creativity and Innovation, Critical Thinking and Problem Solving, ICT Literacy

ISTE/NETS:
Creativity and innovation A, B, C, D

Communication and collaboration A, B, C

Digital citizenship A, B, C, D

Technology operations and concepts A, B, C, D

Fun & Excitement:

Enjoying what you are doing whether at work, school, or play.

Objective:

Students will be able to effectively utilize Twitter to increase their own engagement and interest. Students will be able to formulate Tweets related to a learning concept.

Steps:

- Make sure each student has access to a Twitter account or creates an account. A student who does not want to create a Twitter account may partner up with a peer.
- With students, pick one of the following ways to use Twitter to be engaging or relevant:
  - Twitter class chat: Use Twitter to have a class discussion on a concept you are studying. Have students come up with a creative hashtag to use. Create an archive of the conversation by using Storify.
  - Find live Tweeting of a concept that you are teaching about. For example, a holocaust survivor guest speaker with a live Tweet session or live Tweeting of a surgery. Students can join in the conversation.
  - Follow several accounts relevant to a topic you are studying. Students can ask questions to experts in the field of study. Synthesize the information into a report.
  - Search a vocabulary word or concept and see how others around the world use the term.
  - During direct instruction, students can live Tweet comments, their opinions, and questions via their device to a real-time feed displayed at the front of the class.
  - Have students live Tweet a book or movie.

> **Twitter Assignment: #scientific revolution**
>
> Make a fake Twitter account for one of the scientists during the scientific revolution. Please use your notes and other reputable Internet websites to Tweet five interesting facts. Be sure to have an appropriate/creative hashtag corresponding with the topic.
>
> For example:
>
> @francisbacon could Tweet: All scientists should proceed from the particular to the general by making systematic observations and test these theories. #hungryforscience #inductivereasoning
>
> Interact with other "scientists" by mentioning them in your Tweets!

- Connect with other high school classrooms.
- Create a Twitter account for a historical or literary figure. Be sure that your Tweets match the historical or literary context. Consider tone and language.
- Gather real world data and facts.
- Progressive story—Have students create a story in 140 characters sections. One student writes a bit of the story and then passes it on. The student writing should mention the next student who will add on to the story, and so on.
- Send and translate Tweets in different languages.
- Paraphrase class concepts using 140 characters or explain a concept all in emojis.

Personal Reflection:

Have students complete these sentences:

- I think school is fun when . . .
- I am engaged in learning when . . .

Ask: Why do you think having the condition of Fun & Excitement in your life helps support your aspirations?

Group Discussion:

- Did utilizing Twitter increase student engagement in our class? What other strategies would you like to try in class to increase student engagement?
- What does it mean to have fun at school?
- What could students do to decrease their own boredom at school?

Extended Learning:

Extreme Lesson Make Over: Have students take a subject or assignment that they find boring. Next, ask them to identify why they were not engaged. Then, invite them to come up with a way to learn the material that would be interesting. They should try to connect the material with a hobby or interest they have. Have students share their lesson redesign with the whole class.

Menu

(30–50 MINUTES)

Fun & Excitement:

Enjoying what you are doing whether at work, school, or play.

Objective:

Students will be able to reflect and evaluate their own engagement during a new learning experience.

Steps:

Explain to students that you are trying something new to make class more fun and exciting while still learning.

Pick a new learning activity or strategy from the menu below:

- **Tag Team Debate:** Generate a list of hot topics related to your content. Divide the students into two groups. Each group is to debate either in favor or against the topic but does not get to choose their side. Arrange six chairs in two rows of three, facing each other. Arbitrarily assign students to either the pro or con side. Each side chooses three people to start the debate. Only those seated in the debate chairs can speak. Let other team member's tag in or debate after two minutes. Make sure everyone gets a turn participating.

- **Movie-Making Madness:** Have students create a movie poster that illustrates a concept you are teaching. Students also can create an iMovie trailer. Students can pick the theme and create a movie title and various words to build interest for the upcoming movie featuring your content. If you have shown a movie in class, have students pretend to be the director and create a behind the scenes making the movie video where they reveal their insights and perspectives.

- **Visual Discovery:** To introduce a new topic, show a picture. The picture should be directly related to your content and it should be interesting: unusual, full of emotion, dramatic, funny, witty, or complicated. Scaffold students to figure out what is going on in the image. Then, connect it to your content.

- **Imaginary Field Trip:** Spark student interest by having a school bus picture displayed on the screen. Next play a game on the bus and build suspense! Act like it is a real field trip—review proper behavior and make sure you have emergency medical forms! When you have arrived, display a picture of yourself or the class photoshopped into another setting, time period, for example. Enhance the experience by playing relevant music. Have students use their imaginations and write a journal entry about their field trip. Be sure to pick a field trip to a place that would not be realistic to go to typically!

Source: Photo by Julie Hellerstein.

- **Theme Party:** Plan a theme party where students dress up related to your content. Have students bring in concept-related props and food, for example. At the party, have students socialize about different concepts or play a review game.

- **Act It Out:** Use impromptu and scripted acting to teach a concept. Students can use role cards and act out a scenario. Toward the end of a unit, invite students to do an impromptu skit. Students can also write a script. Props or costumes can enhance this learning strategy.

- **The Big Event:** Ask students to re-create an important concept or theme by turning it into an event of some kind. For example, they can turn a math lesson into a sporting event, a history lesson into a press conference, or a reading assignment into a grand opening.

- **Remix:** Have students rewrite words to a popular song to be about the concept you are studying. Invite students to make a music video to go along with it!

Personal Reflection:

Have students evaluate their engagement level during any one of the activities above.

- They should write a rationale on their interest level by providing details on their actions and feelings.

- Next, have them reflect on a time that they were so engaged doing an activity or learning that they lost track of time.

- Ask: What does it feel like to be so engaged that you lose track of time? How can you improve your own engagement?

Group Reflection:

- What made this lesson engaging or effective?
- What lessons do you find interesting?
- What school subject is especially interesting to you? What is it about the subject that engages you?

Extended Learning:

Create a suggestion box where students can write down suggestions to increase student engagement. Read and discuss the suggestions with the class. Consider these ideas while planning future lessons. Invite a student to plan and teach a lesson.

Notes:

_____

_____

_____

_____

_____

_____

_____

_____

_____

_____

_____

Learning That Sticks

(30–40 MINUTES)

Fun & Excitement:

Enjoying what you are doing whether at work, school, or play. Engaging students is the key to Fun & Excitement. Students learn better and enjoy learning more when they are actively involved in whatever they are learning.

Objective:

Students will be able to express curricular concepts in an unconventional way.

Materials:

Craft sticks and glue; devices with Hyperlapse app.

Steps:

- Warm-up discussion: What does a student look like when he or she is fully involved in an activity? Have students strike a pose and act out what a student would look like. Discuss what they are portraying. What does a student that is fully involved in an activity sound like? Have students call out some examples of what you might hear an engaged student say. Discuss these. What does it feel like to be fully involved in an activity? What does it means to be excited about learning?

- Pass out a craft stick to each student. Have the students write their names on the stick. Collect the sticks. Next, randomly draw sticks to create heterogeneous small groups of three or four students.

- Ask students to create a team name and share their favorite kind of ice pop treat to break the ice. Next, tell the students that they are going to explain a concept that the class has been studying.

- Pick a subject that the class has been studying. Give each group of students twenty minutes to represent their knowledge by using the sticks. Students may not write words.

Common Core:
CCSS.ELA-LITERACY.SL.9-10.5
Make strategic use of digital media (e.g., textual, graphical, audio, visual, and interactive elements) in presentations to enhance understanding of findings, reasoning, and evidence and to add interest.

21st Century Skills:
Initiative and Self-Direction, Collaboration, Creativity and Innovation, Media Literacy

ISTE/NETS:
Creativity and innovation B
Communication and collaboration D
Technology operations and concepts A, D

- While students work on their projects, open up the Hyperlapse app on your smartphone or tablet. Record students. The app automatically speeds up the video. Save the video and show your students what engagement looks like!
- Invite students to share their work with the class.
- Finally, project the video and discuss.

Personal Reflection:

- Did you find you were fully engaged in this style of learning? Why or Why not?
- What ideas do you have for making school work more engaging for you?

Group Reflection:

- What makes building and creating fun? Brainstorm other opportunities for Fun & Excitement that increase student learning.
- What does Fun & Excitement while learning look like? Sound like? Feel like?

Extended Learning:

Students should create their own Hyperlapse movies to illustrate a concept and show progression and growth or movement. Encourage students to research examples such as repairing a phone, crowds of people gathering, students moving in the hallway, cookies baking in an oven, cleaning your room, an airplane taking off, clouds drifting, a plant growing.

Notes:

_____

_____

_____

_____

_____

_____

_____

_____

Heads Up!

(ABOUT 30 MINUTES)

Fun & Excitement:

Enjoying what you are doing whether at work, school, or play. Engaging students is the key to Fun & Excitement. Students learn better and enjoy learning more when they are actively involved in whatever they are learning.

Objective:

Students will be able to recall and describe class concepts to a classmate in an efficient and quick manner. Students will be able to suggest ways to make learning more engaging and fun.

Materials:

iPads or iPhones with Heads Up! app ($0.99); add the build your own deck feature ($0.99). You may decide to give each group an iTunes gift card and they will enter the code on their device or ask for volunteers to buy the app (with parental permission). If you are using a school set of devices, check protocols with your IT department.

> **Common Core:**
> CCSS.ELA-LITERACY.SL.7.1.C
> Pose questions that elicit elaboration and respond to others' questions and comments with relevant observations and ideas that bring the discussion back on topic as needed.
>
> **21st Century Skills:**
> Collaboration, Communication, Creativity and Innovation, Critical Thinking and Problem Solving
>
> **ISTE/NETS:**
> Creativity and innovation A, B, D
> Critical thinking, problem solving, and decision making A, B, C

Steps:

- Explain to students that they are going to review for a test or quiz in an interactive, engaging way.
- Provide students a list of key concepts and vocabulary words or have students create a comprehensive list as a class.
- Students should get into groups of four. Each group should have one device with the Heads Up! app. Watch Ellen DeGeneres's video tutorial of the game. She explains that you pick a category or your own deck.
- How the game works: The person who is guessing first will hold up the device to his or her forehead. Other group members will give the student clues so he or she can guess the word. Students have sixty seconds to get as many words as possible.
- To begin playing, have students open the Heads Up! app. They should click Build Your Own Deck and create their deck by entering the words from the list generated earlier.

- Begin playing the game.
- The front camera and a mobile device records the whole session. After a round, have students watch the video of them explaining each word.
- Ask students to take turns and see who can get the most words correct in one minute.

Source: © Goodluz/Thinkstock Photos

Personal Reflection:

- Describe your engagement in this activity. Was it fun? How did you contribute to the fun? How could you make school more interesting?
- When do you find learning fun? When are you most engaged in learning?

Group Reflection:

Using a Google document or another collaborative list, have students share their ideas on how to improve learning in the classroom. Have a discussion on what makes learning fun and how to make something that is boring more exciting. Have students respond to each other's points and make relevant observations on the topic.

Extended Learning:

Invite students to work in teams to create a new learning review game using the appropriate classroom content. Encourage students to be creative. Students can incorporate physical activity, art, hands-on learning, competition, technology, and more to make it engaging. Next, have students teach other students how to play their game.

Notes:

_____

_____

_____

_____

_____

_____

Appy Hour

(40–50 MINUTES)

Fun & Excitement:

Enjoying what you are doing whether at work, school, or play. Engaging students is the key to Fun & Excitement. Students learn better and enjoy learning more when they are actively involved in whatever they are learning.

Objective:

Students will be able to present and teach on effective studying and learning applications and strategies.

Materials:

Devices with access to app store, Internet, Apple TV or projector for displaying.

Steps:

- Warm-up discussion about engagement and technology: Is technology a distraction to learning or a learning tool? How can technology increase your learning? When have you used technology in school? How have you learned with technology outside of the classroom?

- Ask students to research apps and technology that increase student learning such as review games, educational programs, note-taking apps, creation apps, interactive programs, or video games.

- Students should pick one app or strategy to teach to the class. Students need to demonstrate how to use the app and explain how it makes learning more fun. Students should explain how the app helps them directly with classroom content.

- Next hold "Appy Hour." Invite students to present one app or technology strategy that helps them learn. Students should explain key features of the app and how it helps them be engaged and learn. Have each student present at the front of the class and connect their device to the projector. Have students celebrate after each presentation. You may decide to serve apple juice and apple snacks to make it like a restaurant Happy Hour.

> **Common Core:**
> CCSS.ELA-LITERACY.SL.7.1
> Engage effectively in a range of collaborative discussions.
> CCSS.ELA-LITERACY.SL.8.4
> Present claims and findings, emphasizing salient points in a focused, coherent manner with relevant evidence, sound valid reasoning, and well-chosen details; use appropriate eye contact, adequate volume, and clear pronunciation.
>
> **21st Century Skills:**
> Critical Thinking and Problem Solving, Communication, Collaboration, Media Literacy, Information Literacy
>
> **ISTE/NETS:**
> Creativity and innovation A, B
> Communication and collaboration A, B, D
> Critical thinking, problem solving, and decision making A, B, C, D
> Digital citizenship B
> Technology operations and concepts B

- Allow time for questions and answers.
- Encourage students to use these apps while studying or try to incorporate them into your classroom practices.

Personal Reflection:

- Ask students to take a screen shot of their app and provide a summary of what the app does and how it connects to learning.
- Ask: What makes this app fun and interesting? Did this assignment change your perspective on the relationship between technology and learning?

Group Reflection:

Students can share their screen shots and summaries onto a classroom blog or forum like Edmodo. Students can post questions and comments about each app.

- What does it feel like to have fun at school?
- How do you see students enjoying learning?
- Why do you think school is boring at times?
- What can you do today to be more engaged in your learning at school?

Extended Learning:

Discuss the learning apps. What characteristics did they share? Did some require higher levels of thinking? Could you combine any features to make a super-learning app? As a class, come up with a new learning app that helps students understand what they are currently studying in class. Have them name the app, design the icon, and write a short description of what it does. Students who are interested in technology could proceed to make the app. There are many resources online to help.

Notes:

_____

_____

_____

_____

_____

Un-Bored Games

(ABOUT 40 MINUTES)

Fun & Excitement:

Enjoying what you are doing whether at work, school, or play. Engaging students is the key to Fun & Excitement. Perhaps nothing is more fun and exciting for students than to mix up rules and do things differently.

Objective:

Students will be able to modify existing rules to a board game. Students will be able to construct a new classroom rule that increases student engagement.

Materials:

One board game or card game for every four students or online board games from http://www.pogo.com/board-games or another gaming site.

> **Common Core:**
> CCSS.ELA-LITERACY.SL.6-8.1
> Engage effectively in a range of collaborative discussions.
>
> **21st Century Skills:**
> Critical Thinking and Problem Solving, Creativity and Innovation, Communication, Collaboration
>
> **ISTE/NETS:**
> Creativity and innovation A, B
>
> Communication and collaboration A, B, D
>
> Critical thinking, problem solving, and decision making A, B, C, D

Steps:

- Have students bring in board or card games. These can be online or traditional games.
- Warm-up discussion: What subjects and assignments do you find fun and exciting at school? Explain.
- Post a list of school rules or your classroom rules. What rules do you think get in the way of school being a more exciting place for learning? Why do you think these rules prevent fun?
- Divide students into random groups of three or four by using playing cards. You can match students based on suit or number depending on what works best with your number of students.
- Each group should pick a familiar board game and rewrite the rules of the game that they selected to make it even more fun.
- Instruct students to write out the new directions and new rules.
- Allow students to play their new game and share the new rules with the entire class.

Personal Reflection:

- Why do you think changing the rules of a game makes playing that game more fun?
- What rule changes would make professional sports more fun to watch?
- What new rules would promote Fun & Excitement in this class?

Group Reflection:

Students will think-pair-share with their responses from their personal reflection. Discuss what new rules would promote Fun & Excitement in this class. As a class, select one rule to implement that would increase student engagement for all students. Be sure to think through all of the implications for this rule. Add the rule to the syllabus. Have students brainstorm ways to enforce this rule.

Extended Learning:

What new rules would promote Fun & Excitement in school? Critically evaluate the student handbook rules for your school based on student learning and Fun & Excitement. Pick two rules. How do these rules promote or hinder Fun & Excitement for students? Write a rationale. Next, rewrite one rule to increase Fun & Excitement at school. If your new rule was in effect, how do you predict students would behave? How would this impact school faculty and students?

Research social contract theory. Use primary sources to guide discussion. Why are rules important for society? What rules promote social order? Who should benefit from rules or laws? What rules and laws in our government would you like to see changed? Explain an idea for a law that would increase Fun & Excitement in the workplace or schools.

Notes:

_____

_____

_____

_____

_____

_____

_____

CHAPTER 5

Curiosity & Creativity

The last thirty minutes of monthly staff meetings at one high school end with excitement and anticipation. In a hat are the names of the eight departments in the school: math, science, social studies, language arts, foreign language, the arts (which include fine and performing arts), technology, and physical education. At the end of the meeting, department chairs draw a slip from the hat. If they draw their own department (or one they drew the previous month), they must try again. Whatever department they select commits half of their department to do interdisciplinary work with. The other half of the department will work with whatever department draws *their* name. The science chair may draw foreign language, but then the art chair may draw science. Among themselves, the science teachers decide who will work with foreign language teachers and who will work with art teachers. The remainder of the thirty minutes is spent sketching the interdepartmental work that lies ahead. Teachers have found new energy and enthusiasm working with colleagues across departments and the students are the ultimate beneficiaries of lessons that are both creative and engaging.

Curious students ask "Why?" Creative students ask "Why not?" While this may oversimplify two very complex realities, curiosity and creativity are paid far too little attention in schools given their importance to lifelong learning and successful living. Despite the number of educators, business people, and politicians that are beating the drum for students to become inquisitive and innovative, to have probing and flexible minds, the educational landscape is still dominated by a common core, common standards, common curricula, and common assessments.

Curiosity & Creativity is about intellectual engagement. Specifically, both curiosity and creativity are products of an engaged imagination. The ability to wonder—in a way that leads to questions and creations—may be a uniquely human capacity. It is the driving force behind both science and art. It is the impulse behind understanding and invention. When students are able to relate what they are learning to material they have previously learned, to other subjects, and to the world around them, they become more engaged. When they can use their inborn desire to be creative to develop new ways of thinking and doing they become absorbed in whatever it is they are doing.

No one doubts the critical importance of teaching students to ask and pursue good questions. And very few people (though some do) argue about the importance of teaching students to be original, creative, and innovative. Yet classes that encourage creativity like art and music are cut or shortened to make room for so-called "core" subjects. And within those core subjects themselves, student inquiry and questioning is fairly limited by the dictates of the curriculum and what will be on the test. We have talked with students who as early as middle school are craving electives that would allow them to pursue their interests and curiosities. How sad is it that in the 2014 national results for the Student Voice Survey, Quaglia Institute for Student Aspirations (QISA) reports 78% of sixth graders agree with the statement, "At school I am encouraged to be creative" but by twelfth grade just 62% of students agree with that same statement?

The following activities are intended to reverse this trend by helping teachers and students tap their sense of wonder. The exercises invite you to stretch your imagination to become more inquisitive and inventive. The routine of school sometimes can lead to a same-old-same-old dulling of the ability to question and create. By engaging in these playful experiences of Curiosity & Creativity, you will help your students develop habits that support their learning for a lifetime.

Blackout Poetry

(ABOUT 50 MINUTES)

Curiosity & Creativity:

Asking "Why?" and "Why not?" about the world around you.

Objective:

Students will be able to create original poetry by deconstructing a page of text.

Materials:

Projector and Internet to show examples; newspapers, book pages, photocopies, articles for every student; black markers or pens.

Steps:

- Warm-up discussion: Can being creative allow you to see ordinary things differently? Explain.

- Explain to students that they are going to think differently and creatively for this assignment. Writer and artist Austin Kleon has encouraged people to create poetry from ordinary text. Show examples of Austin Kleon's work from the Web at http://austinkleon.com/newspaperblackout/.

- As a class, practice creating digital black out poetry. Click on the following link: http://www.nytimes.com/interactive/2014/multimedia/blackout-poetry.html. Have the class scan the article on the left hand side. Ask the class what word stands out to them. When you click on the word on the article on the left side, it shows up highlighted on the right hand side. By highlighting words, create a short poem as a class. Students can continue to make their own digital poems by using the link.

- Students should then create their own blackout poetry.
  - Each student should use a piece of text. You may encourage students to bring in their own text: newspapers, pages of books, or any print articles. Bring in a variety of texts for students to choose from. You may decide to have students use a text that is relevant to your current unit of study or allow students to use any text.

> **Common Core:**
> CCSS.ELA-LITERACY.W.9-10.6
> Use technology, including the Internet, to produce, publish, and update individual or shared writing products, taking advantage of technology's capacity to link to other information and to display information flexibly and dynamically.
> CCSS.ELA-LITERACY.W.11-12.3.D
> Use precise words and phrases, telling details, and sensory language to convey a vivid picture of the experiences, events, setting, and/or characters.
>
> **21st Century Skills:**
> Creativity and Innovation
>
> **ISTE/NETS:**
> Creativity and innovation A, B

Source: Courtesy of Jessica Hellerstein.

- ○ Remind students to be relaxed and creative. This assignment is just about thinking differently.
- ○ Students should remember that the poem would be read left to right and top to bottom. Students should scan the article and look for words that jump out at them.
- ○ Next, students can read the full text looking for connecting words. Once the words for the poem are identified, students should black out the unwanted words in each line.
- ○ Invite students to turn their poem into an illustration by doodling.
- Share the poetry in a way that your class prefers.
  - ○ Allow students to read their poetry aloud to the class.
  - ○ Hang up poems on a bulletin board.
  - ○ Take pictures of the poems and post to a class blog or website.
  - ○ Post pictures of poems on Instagram or Facebook or create a #blackoutpoetry class specific hashtag. Allow students to search the hashtags to see their peer's poems.

Personal Reflection:

- How did you change the original meaning of the text?
- What was the article about?
- What does your poem mean?
- What was it like to create your poem?
- What part of your poem are you most proud of?

Group Reflection:

- How did it feel to write poetry?
- What was it like to see and hear your peer's poetry?
- How can we foster creativity in this class?

Extended Learning:

Students can create a Pinterest board dedicated to creativity and poetry. Using Pinterest, students can pin and collect their favorite blackout poetry or other poems. They can also upload their own original work.

Notes:

_____

_____

_____

_____

_____

_____

_____

_____

_____

_____

_____

Genius Hour/Passion Project

(TO BE DETERMINED BY TEACHER/SEVERAL CLASS PERIODS)

Common Core:

CCSS.ELA-LITERACY.WHST.9-10.7

Conduct short as well as more sustained research projects to answer a question (including a self-generated question) or solve a problem; narrow or broaden the inquiry when appropriate; synthesize multiple sources on the subject, demonstrating understanding of the subject under investigation.

21st Century Skills:

Critical Thinking and Problem Solving, Creativity and Innovation, Collaboration, Initiative and Self-Direction, Productivity and Accountability

ISTE/NETS:

Creativity and innovation B

Communication and collaboration A

Research and information fluency B, C, D

Critical thinking, problem solving, and decision making A, B, C, D

Curiosity & Creativity:

Asking "Why?" and "Why not?" about the world around you. Students will have the freedom to explore and research what they are passionate about.

Objective:

Students will be able to form a driving question, organize research, compose a presentation, and share their findings about a topic they are passionate about.

Materials:

Devices or computers for students; materials will vary depending on student project.

Steps:

- Before introducing the assignment, decide on guidelines for the project in your classroom.
    - How much time will students have for their projects? Some Genius Hour teachers recommend one hour per week. Some teachers provide students with 20% time.
    - Design benchmarks and reflections for students. Search Genius Hour on the Web for more information.
    - Modify an existing rubric or create a rubric that meets your needs.
- Warm-up discussion: What is something you have always wanted to learn about? Why are you curious about that?
- Provide students an overview of Genius Hour by showing the following video at https://www.youtube.com/watch?v=NMFQUtHsWhc.

- Invite students to focus on their own passions, interests, and talents. Allow students ample time to brainstorm ideas for their passion project. If a student is struggling to list interests, students could list five to ten things that they love to do, five to ten things they are curious about, and five to ten things that they are good at.
- Have students answer the following project proposal questions:
  - What is your proposed topic? List your driving question.
  - Why is this question important to you?
  - What do you hope to learn?
  - What kind of research do you think will help you?
  - What materials will you need?
  - How will you plan to share your project?
  - How can the teacher and other students support you in your project?
- Have students work with a partner to refine their inquiry-based driving question. Check to be sure questions have sufficient depth and breadth. Once the question is well formed, instruct students to begin researching.
- Explain to students that the project must involve research. Specify research guidelines.
- Upon completion, projects should be shared with the class and in a global way. Also encourage students to share their project in a creative way. Students must also explain the process of their passion project.

Personal Reflection:

- Why can researching your own question sometimes be more interesting than researching questions a teacher assigns?
- What was the most rewarding part of your passion project?
- What was the most challenging part?

Group Reflection:

- "You are a genius. The world expects your contribution." What are you teaching the world? How did your projects help teach the world?
- What did you learn from your classmates? View *Kid President's Pep Talk to Teachers and Students!* video at https://www.youtube.com/watch?v=RwlhUcSGqgs.

Extended Learning:

Students will share their projects, insights, challenges, successes, and recommendations on Twitter. Students can participate in a live Twitter chat and share their projects to other teachers by using the hashtag #geniushour.

Marshmallow Challenge

(ABOUT 50 MINUTES)

Curiosity & Creativity:

Asking "Why?" and "Why not?" about the world around you. Students will use creative thinking skills to build a tall structure out of uncooked spaghetti, string, marshmallow, and tape.

Objective:

Students will be able to use creative thinking skills and collaborate with peers to build a structure out of random objects.

Materials:

A marshmallow challenge kit for each team: twenty sticks of spaghetti, one yard of masking tape, one yard of string, and one marshmallow. These ingredients should be placed into a paper lunch bag.

Steps:

- Prior to the activity, have students go to http://marshmallow challenge.com/Instructions.html for step-by-step instructions on set up, directions, and more helpful hints.
- Form groups of four students.
- Begin the challenge.
- To debrief, show this video at http://www.ted.com/talks/tom_wujec_build_a_tower.

Personal Reflection:

- How did you use creative thinking during this exercise?
- Describe a real-life situation where you used creative thinking.
- How did your team collaborate?
- Describe a real-life situation where you collaborated.

> **Common Core:**
> CCSS.ELA-LITERACY.SL.6-8.1
> Engage effectively in a range of collaborative discussions (one-on-one, in groups, and teacher-led) with diverse partners on grade 6-8 topics, texts, and issues, building on others' ideas and expressing their own clearly.
>
> **21st Century Skills:**
> Critical Thinking and Problem Solving, Creativity and Innovation, Collaboration
>
> **ISTE/NETS:**
> Creativity and innovation A
> Communication and collaboration D
> Critical thinking, problem solving, and decision making B

Group Reflection:

- What skills did you use during the marshmallow challenge?
- What roles did everyone take on?
- Why is having diverse skills important?
- How did the different structures vary?

Extended Learning:

Students should use their curiosity and creative thinking skills as they take apart a toy and create a new, unique invention. Students will bring in a toy they no longer play with and dissect their doll, remote control airplane, or plush toy. Next, students should use the parts to create a new, unique toy. Visit http://tinkering.exploratorium.edu/toy-take-apart.

Notes:
_____
_____
_____
_____
_____
_____
_____
_____
_____
_____
_____
_____

CHAPTER 6

Spirit of Adventure

More and more schools have a robotics class. In most schools, this is an elective taken by the most engineer-minded and technically talented students in the school. One school decided to make it a required class. In that class, challenges and risks abound. Those who are gear heads are challenged to find clear and polite ways to explain difficult technical concepts to their less technically sophisticated peers. Those same peers are challenged not just to grasp what is being taught but also to make a contribution to their team given their own talents and strengths. Artists sketch plans articulated by the techies, entrepreneurs develop marketing plans for their team's inventions, wordsmiths write training manuals, photographers document the project, and number crunchers crunch numbers. Along the way, everyone learns to write just enough code to understand and appreciate the complexity behind nearly everything in the modern world. At this school, all students are becoming prepared for the nearly here world of automated cars and robotic surgery.

One of our favorite quotes is from Helen Keller: "Life is either a daring adventure or nothing at all." Out on the very edge of what we are capable of and at the limits of our insights and skills, there is a horizon called *learning*. And it is infinite in scope. That is to say, if we are willing to push ourselves, to move beyond our comfort zones, to take risks, there is no limit to what we can come to understand and know and discover. The adventure of learning is what brought Marco Polo to the East, van Gogh to his canvas, and NASA to the moon. Daring makes it all possible.

Sadly, we have been in schools and talked with students who do not dare to dare. Students tell us they are afraid to answer a question for fear of looking stupid. Others tell us they are afraid to answer a question for fear of looking smart. Some students are afraid to fail, while others are afraid to succeed. "If I do well on a test," one student told us, "they'll expect me to do that well every time." The fact of the matter is that while we have done well with making it safe to make mistakes, we have not yet made it entirely safe in school to be successful. Despite the future earning potential of nerds and geeks, they are still made fun of in many schools.

The challenge for Spirit of Adventure is the individualized nature of risk-taking behavior. Some people are risk seekers; others are risk averse. Some people will try anything; others prefer the tried and true. We have observed classes where some students are leaping out of their seats to read aloud, while others are leaving their seats to go to the restroom in the hopes of not being asked to read aloud. It is one of the trickier parts of being a skilled teacher: knowing when to push a student and when to provide security. But there is no denying that little learning takes place when a student is panicked or overly comfortable. Learning takes place when students are being challenged.

The exercises in this chapter will help you and your students find that sweet spot. Students will learn what it feels like to challenge themselves beyond their comfort zones, but short of their panic zones. Students will be invited to take risks in the safety of the activity and the fun of trying new experiences together. By taking on the healthy risks created by the exercise, they will learn how learning itself is an adventure.

Student-Led Help Desk

(ABOUT 50 MINUTES AND FOLLOW-UP)

Spirit of Adventure:

Being excited to try new things, even if you don't know you'll excel.

Objective:

Students will be able to plan a strategy to implement a student-led help desk for technology or Genius Bar for their school. Students will be able to troubleshoot systems and applications.

Materials:

The article "The Genius Bar Goes to School—Generation YES" (available at http://genyes.org/files/staticcontent/genius_bar .pdf).

Steps:

- Brainstorm: Do you notice that people get frustrated with technology often? How can we encourage others that it is okay to make a mistake while using technology? How can we share basic tips and address basic problems?

- What app or computer system did you find difficult at first? List these on the board. How did you overcome this?

- Research student-led genius bars online. Have students share examples and different models. Read the genyes.org article.

- How could we adapt this model at our school?

- What resources would we need to establish a Genius Bar? When could it be open—at lunch, before school, or after school?

- What adults will we need to partner with us? How will it benefit students? How could we help teachers who are less familiar with technology?

- How can we recruit tech savvy students? How can we use other students' skills? (as customer service, PR, etc.) What new skills will Genius Bar helpers need to possess?

- Write a proposal and share this idea with the principal.

Common Core:
CCSS.ELA-LITERACY.SL.9-12.1.C
Propel conversations by posing and responding to questions that relate the current discussion to broader themes or larger ideas; actively incorporate others into the discussion; and clarify, verify, or challenge ideas and conclusions.

CCSS.ELA-LITERACY.SL.9-12.1
Initiate and participate effectively in a range of collaborative discussions (one-on-one, in groups, and teacher-led) with diverse partners on grades 9-12 topics, texts, and issues, building on others' ideas and expressing their own clearly and persuasively.

21st Century Skills:
Critical Thinking and Problem Solving, Communication, Collaboration, Leadership and Responsibility, Flexibility and Adaptability, ICT Literacy

ISTE/NETS:
Critical thinking, problem solving, and decision making B, D

Communication and collaboration D

Technology, operations, and concepts A, C, D

Personal Reflection:

- Identify a tech problem that you do not know how to solve.

- Research potential solutions online.

- Pose a question online or to a classmate. Apply this knowledge and see if it solves your problem. Write a few sentences about your experience.

- How can we encourage perseverance when using new technology among our peers?

- Write a narrative or blog about a time when you showed perseverance in another area of your life. Use pictures to enhance your story.

Group Reflection:

Collaborate with classmates and the IT department at your school to create a student help desk website. What issues should the website address? For example, will you create video tutorials about basic tech issues? Will you include student resources? Teacher resources? Student-written app reviews? Check out Burlington High School Help Desk at http://bhshelpdesk.com.

Extended Learning:

Have students invite peers to guest blog about making mistakes and perseverance. What was the result?

Notes:

_____

_____

_____

_____

_____

_____

_____

In the Zone

(40–50 MINUTES)

Spirit of Adventure:

Spirit of Adventure is about challenging yourself to grow. We rarely learn when materials or situations are too easy or too difficult. Figuring out where your comfort, challenge, and panic zones are can help you learn.

Objective:

Students will be able to categorize their experiences into three different zones: comfort, challenge, and panic. Students will be able to evaluate a challenging experience and their learning.

Materials:

Three large pieces of newsprint and markers; devices with photo-editing apps for extended learning.

Steps:

- Warm-up discussion: What does it mean to challenge yourself? Why are some people able to take more risks than others?

- Place three pieces of newsprint in different corners of the room with the headings: COMFORT ZONE, CHALLENGE ZONE, and PANIC ZONE.

- Give students a brief description of each zone.
  - Comfort Zone: Things are easy for you, your skills are completely equal to or exceed the task at hand, your heart rate is even and breathing is easy—for example, reading to your younger sibling.
  - Challenge Zone: Things are more difficult but not unworkable. Your skills are stretched, your heart rate picks up, and you may take a deep breath—for example, reading aloud to the class when the subject matter is new.

Common Core:

CCSS.ELA-LITERACY.W.9-12.3
Write narratives to develop real or imagined experiences or events using effective technique, well-chosen details, and well-structured event sequences.

CCSS.ELA-LITERACY.W.9-12.3.A
Engage and orient the reader by setting out a problem, situation, or observation, establishing one or multiple point(s) of view, and introducing a narrator and/or characters; create a smooth progression of experiences or events.

CCSS.ELA-LITERACY.W.9-12.3.B
Use narrative techniques, such as dialogue, pacing, description, reflection, and multiple plot lines, to develop experiences, events, and/or characters.

CCSS.ELA-LITERACY.SL.9-12.1
Initiate and participate effectively in a range of collaborative discussions (one-on-one, in groups, and teacher-led) with diverse partners on grades 9-12 topics, texts, and issues, building on others' ideas and expressing their own clearly and persuasively.

21st Century Skills:
Creativity and Innovation, Critical Thinking and Problem Solving, Initiative and Self-Direction

o Panic Zone: Things seem impossible and completely over your head. Your reaction is to resist or run. Your breathing is short and your heart pounds—for example, memorizing a poem and reciting it to the whole school.

- Students will go to each corner and write down examples and real-life experiences for each zone.

- Debrief with students after all have finished. Did you notice that what was comfortable for one person might be a challenge for another, or even a panic zone?

Personal Reflection:

- Write a narrative about one of your experiences in your challenge zone.

- Why was this activity in your challenge zone? How did you feel?

- How did this impact your learning?

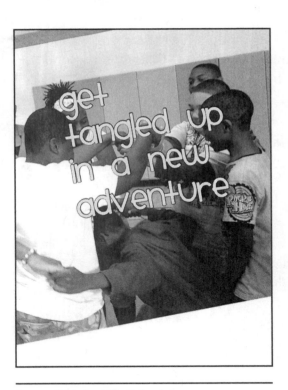

Source: Photo by Julie Hellerstein.

Group Reflection:

- Why do you think the same activities create comfort for some, challenge for some, and panic for some? Give an example.

  With a small group, answer the following questions:

- What would it take for you to move an activity in your comfort zone to challenge zone? What would it take for you to move an activity in your panic zone to your challenge zone?

Extended Learning:

Have students create a motivational poster or Internet meme to encourage students to have a Spirit of Adventure and push themselves to take on challenges in their challenge zone. Students can use apps like Meme Something, PicCollage, or A Beautiful Mess.

I Dare You Cards

(10–15 MINUTES; 20 MINUTE FOLLOW-UP SEVERAL DAYS LATER)

Spirit of Adventure:

Being excited to try new things, even if you don't know if you'll excel.

Objective:

Students will be able to accept and reflect on a challenge that requires a Spirit of Adventure.

Materials:

Sticky notes for every student.

Steps:

- Warm-up discussion: Why is it important to have a Spirit of Adventure in life and school?
- Tell students that they are going to dare each other to have a Spirit of Adventure in a healthy way. Students should write Adventure Actions on sticky notes and stick them on the board. Examples can be:
  - Read a book from a new genre. For example, if non-fiction is your thing, try a romance novel.
  - Order something unique off the menu at a restaurant.
  - If you drive, take a different route home than your normal route (but stay safe).
  - Walk up to someone in the lunchroom that you have never met before and strike up a conversation.
  - Wear a unique outfit to school.
  - Ask someone new to be your partner on a project.
  - Share a talent with your teachers.
  - Join a new club.

Common Core:
CCSS.ELA-LITERACY.W.9-12.3
Write narratives to develop real or imagined experiences or events using effective technique, well-chosen details, and well-structured event sequences.

CCSS.ELA-LITERACY.SL.9-12.1
Initiate and participate effectively in a range of collaborative discussions (one-on-one, in groups, and teacher-led) with diverse partners on grades 9-12 topics, texts, and issues, building on others' ideas and expressing their own clearly and persuasively.

21st Century Skills:
Collaboration, Critical Thinking and Problem Solving, Creativity and Innovation

ISTE/NETS:
Digital citizenship B, D

Communication and collaboration A, D

Critical thinking, problem solving, and decision making B

- o Enter a competition that you may not excel in.
- o Switch up your daily routine. Work out in the morning instead of at night.
- o Take part in a dance off.
- Allow students to go up to the board and accept an Adventure Action card.
- Have students read their Adventure Action card aloud. Allow students to give advice, feedback, or tell relevant stories about the actions.

Personal Reflection:

- Students will write an essay about their experience. Describe what Adventure Action you picked.
- What did you do? How did you feel while doing the activity?
- What did this experience teach you?

Group Reflection:

- After completing their actions, students will share reflections in small groups.
- Next, have a whole group discussion on how to encourage someone to take a healthy risk or try something new.
- What is the difference between a healthy risk versus an unhealthy risk? How can you anticipate if a risk will be healthy?
- How can we better support each other when we succeed and also make mistakes?

Extended Learning:

Have students challenge a larger audience to take on an Adventure Challenge. Compile a list of challenges and submit it to the school newspaper. Then, set up a booth at lunch and hand out sticky note challenges. Use Twitter or other social media to challenge students and share what you learned. Be sure to explain why having a Spirit of Adventure increases learning!

Notes:

_____

_____

_____

_____

Student Speak

(50 MINUTES, SPACE OUT STUDENT PRESENTATIONS OVER THE NEXT FEW WEEKS, HAVING 1 OR 2 STUDENTS PRESENT AT A TIME)

Spirit of Adventure:

Being excited to try new things, even if you don't know if you'll excel. Spirit of Adventure encourages students to take healthy risks. This activity encourages students to take risks by providing them with a safe and comfortable environment to share and teach out of their expertise and interest.

Objective:

Students will be able to report on a topic of their choice.

Materials:

Projector; video clip from Google Nexus TV commercial.

Steps:

- Watch the Google Nexus TV commercial at http://www.ispot.tv/ad/7qCq/google-nexus-7-speech.

- Ask students: What does it feel like to speak in front of the class? Does knowing the subject matter well help you speak in front of the class?

- Discuss how students have varied interests and knowledge and how it is important to share their interests.

- Ask students to make a list of things they are interested in and know a lot about.

- Place no limit on what a student may be good at—video games, gaining Instagram followers, knitting, dancing, or knowing where to find clothes on sale, for example.

- Invite students to create a short presentation or demonstration on their interests and expertise. Allow students to bring in props, visual aids, or do something creative for their presentation.

- Allow students to share their expertise over the course of several weeks.

Common Core:
CCSS.ELA-LITERACY.SL.6-8.4 Present claims and findings, sequencing ideas logically and using pertinent descriptions, facts, and details to accentuate main ideas or themes; use appropriate eye contact, adequate volume, and clear pronunciation.

CCSS.ELA-LITERACY.SL.6-8.5 Include multimedia components (e.g., graphics, images, music, sound) and visual displays in presentations to clarify information.

21st Century Skills:
Communication, Creativity and Innovation, Initiative and Self-Direction

ISTE/NETS:
Research and information fluency A

Communication and collaboration B

Source: Photo by Julie Hellerstein.

Personal Reflection:

- What was it like to talk in front of the class regarding something you were confident about?
- Self-Assessment: Students will score themselves on the following statements: Always, Most of the time, Sometimes, Seldom, Never.

  1. I have someone to talk to when I feel overwhelmed at school.

  2. I try to be successful in all my classes.

  3. I set goals for myself.

  4. I like being challenged at school.

  5. I am not afraid to make mistakes.

  6. I want to be successful.

  7. I push myself to do better in school.

  8. I ask for help when I need it.

Group Reflection:

- Why do you think public speaking is such a big fear for some people? How can we act to reduce this fear?
- Why is it important to speak out and participate in class?
- What are some other common fears?

Extended Learning:

Students will search the Internet and select a public speaking activity for the class to complete. Have the student set up and lead the activity. Here are some examples: http://publicspeakingpower.com/fun-public-speaking-activities/ and http://www.write-out-loud.com/public-speaking-activities.html.

Adventure Advice

(40–50 MINUTES)

Spirit of Adventure:

Being excited to try new things, even if you don't know if you'll excel.

Objective:

Students will be able to write an advice column addressing how to overcome fears and include personal experience.

Materials:

Sticky notes.

Steps:

- Ask students to write advice columns about how to have a Spirit of Adventure and overcome fears.

- Prewrite: Identify a time you were afraid to try something new. What did it feel like to be afraid? What were you afraid of at the time? Remind students to keep these feelings in mind for this assignment.

- Invite students to write down what they are afraid to do both in school and life on a sticky note and post it on the board. Examples can be public speaking, singing in front of a group, striking out at a baseball game, or failing a test.

- Next, have students look at the sticky notes and select a fear that they could give good advice about.

- Students should then write a digital advice column to their peers about their experience overcoming that fear. The student should include advice and different strategies to try. Students should include multimedia images, GIFs, videos, or relevant resource links.

- Compile all the articles into a newsletter.

> **Common Core:**
> CCSS.ELA-LITERACY.W.6-8.2
> Write informative/explanatory texts to examine a topic and convey ideas, concepts, and information through the selection, organization, and analysis of relevant content.
> CCSS.ELA-LITERACY.W.6-8.6
> Use technology, including the Internet, to produce and publish writing and link to and cite sources as well as to interact and collaborate with others, including linking to and citing sources.
>
> **21st Century Skills:**
> Communication, Creativity and Innovation
>
> **ISTE/NETS:**
> Communication and collaboration B
> Creativity and innovation A, B
> Digital citizenship B

Source: Photo by Julie Hellerstein.

- Invite students to present solutions to the class.
- Ask: What steps would you need to take to make your solution possible? Who could you present your idea to? Who would you need to work in partnership with?
- Have students predict the outcome to the solution.

Personal Reflection:

- Describe a time when you offered a solution to an authentic problem.
- What was the outcome? Did you need to work in partnership with anyone?

Group Reflection:

Invite students to pose questions about each solution.

Among these they should ask:

- What resources are needed?
- Who does this benefit?
- Will this solve the issue?

- What are the implications?
- How will we know if the solution worked?

Group members should edit and adapt their plans using helpful feedback.

Extended Learning:

Have students share their solutions to multiple audiences using a variety of media and formats. They should work in partnership with key adults and players to present at a school board meeting or staff meeting and create posters, post ideas on a blog, Twitter, or Instagram.

Notes:

Good, Bad, Horrible Advice

(ABOUT 30 MINUTES)

Leadership & Responsibility:

Making decisions and taking responsibility for your choices. Student leaders can evaluate the quality of different decisions.

Objective:

Students will be able to use critical thinking skills to form different kinds of advice for typical school scenarios.

Materials:

Scenario cards; Edmodo or online forum for extended learning.

Steps:

- Call up three students to the front of the room. Allow one student to pick out one scenario card randomly.
    - Someone drops their books in the hallway.
    - Someone wants to skip class.
    - Someone's brother offers his notebook of all his old tests in your science class.
    - Your teacher recycles the same tests every year.
    - Someone is thinking of getting test answers online.
    - Your friend is copying math homework in study hall.
    - Your teacher marks a test wrong and you get an A instead of a C.
    - In the school parking lot, someone sees a student hand another student a small bag of marijuana and the other student hands him money.
    - Someone sees a student taking another student's iPhone out of her purse when she is in the bathroom.
    - A group of students leave their trash from lunch on the table.

Common Core:
CCSS.ELA-LITERACY.SL.9-12.1
Initiate and participate effectively in a range of collaborative discussions (one-on-one, in groups, and teacher-led) with diverse partners on grades 9-12 topics, texts, and issues, building on others' ideas and expressing their own clearly and persuasively.

CCSS.ELA-LITERACY.W.9-10.10
Write routinely over extended time frames (time for research, reflection, and revision) and shorter time frames (a single sitting or a day or two) for a range of tasks, purposes, and audiences.

21st Century Skills:
Critical Thinking and Problem Solving, Creativity and Innovation, Communication, Leadership and Responsibility

ISTE/NETS:
Critical thinking, problem solving, and decision making D

Communication and collaboration B

Creativity and innovation B

- A fight breaks out in the lunchroom.
- Someone misses her school bus.
- A negative Tweet goes around the school about a teacher.
- Someone is talking back to a staff member.
- Someone is spreading a rumor about your friend.

• Tell the students that the first student should give good advice, the second student should give bad advice, and the third student should give horrible advice.

• Call up the next three students to pick the next scenario. Repeat the procedure so all students can participate.

Personal Reflection:

• Describe a real scenario using fictitious names about when you gave good, bad, or horrible advice. Describe the outcomes.

• With your new insight, what would you do next time in a similar situation?

• Why do leaders need to think about the outcomes of their actions and the advice they give?

Group Reflection:

• Why is it important to think through your actions for different scenarios?

• What makes a responsible leader? What makes an irresponsible leader?

• What traits do you admire most in student leaders?

Extended Learning:

• Using Edmodo, post the following scenarios. Allow students to read and think about the responses. Next, have students write good advice about what the leader should do.

- You have been designated the leader of your group of friends. You did not ask to be the leader, but everyone looks to you whenever it comes time to decide the group's move. Someone in your group is getting involved with issues that could get him in trouble. As a leader, what do you do?

- Your school's student council is a waste of time. Being on the student council is just an excuse to get out of class and a way to make your college application look good. You truly want the opportunity to be a leader. How do you change the student council to make it a true leadership group?

- Your school has decided to cut its after-school programs. Obviously, this development is upsetting to most students. How do you go about doing something to ensure that the students' ideas and opinions are heard by the administration?

• Research and post on Edmodo about some extraordinary student leaders. Comment on your peers' findings. What traits are common? Do student leaders take responsibility for their actions?

Someone drops their books in the hallway.	Someone wants to skip class.	Someone's brother offers his notebook of all his old tests in your science class.
Your teacher recycles the same tests every year.	Someone is thinking of getting test answers online.	Your friend is copying math homework in study hall.
Your teacher marks a test wrong and you get an A instead of a C.	In the school parking lot, someone sees a student hand another student a small bag of marijuana and the other student hands him money.	Someone sees a student taking another student's iPhone out of her purse when she is in the bathroom.
A group of students leave their trash from lunch on the table.	A fight breaks out in the lunchroom.	Someone misses her school bus.
A negative Tweet goes around the school about a teacher.	Someone is talking back to a staff member.	Someone is spreading a rumor about your friend.

Tag Team Debate

(ABOUT 40 MINUTES)

Common Core:
CCSS.ELA-LITERACY.SL.6-8.1
Engage effectively in a range of collaborative discussions (one-on-one, in groups, and teacher-led) with diverse partners on grade 6-8 topics, texts, and issues, building on others' ideas and expressing their own clearly.

CCSS.ELA-LITERACY.SL.6-8.4
Present claims and findings, sequencing ideas logically and using pertinent descriptions, facts, and details to accentuate main ideas or themes; use appropriate eye contact, adequate volume, and clear pronunciation.

21st Century Skills:
Critical Thinking and Problem Solving, Communication, Collaboration

ISTE/NETS:
Critical thinking, problem solving and decision making D

Research and information fluency B, C

Communication and collaboration B, D

Leadership & Responsibility:

Leadership & Responsibility is about students feeling confident voicing their opinions and ideas. This activity encourages students to articulate opinions and listen respectfully to the opinions of others.

Objective:

Students will be able to articulate and voice their opinions while listening respectfully to the opinions of others.

Materials:

Devices with Popplet app for extended learning; six chairs.

Steps:

- What does it feel like to voice and defend an opinion? What is your overall opinion about school?

- Students should write down three controversial school issues that matter to students. This might include the dress code, homework policy, and discipline rules.

- Have the class resolve each of the issues into a statement—for example, "There should be a more relaxed dress code." "There should be no homework."

- Select one of the statements and randomly assign teams to make arguments either in favor of the statement (pro) or against it (con). Assign a third group as observers. Students need not actually agree with the position they are defending.

- Give students five to ten minutes to develop sound points in defense of the opinion their group must support. Have the observers anticipate the arguments others will make.

- Allow the pro and con groups to debate the issue by each putting forward their students to start the debate. Set up three chairs facing another three chairs. Other students on the team can have a seat at the debate table by tapping one of their classmates on the shoulder and taking their place. Only three students from each team can be debating at one time.
- After each debate, ask observers which side was more effective and why.
- Repeat with other topics. Rotate the groups so observers have a chance to debate.
- Make sure everyone gets a turn participating.

Personal Reflection:

- What was it like to argue for a position you do not agree with? What was it like to argue a position you do agree with?
- What did you learn from being an observer?
- Why do leaders need to consider both sides of an argument? Describe a situation when you considered both sides before making a decision.

Group Reflection:

What was difficult? What suggestions were most appealing? What would have helped the debate be stronger? Did anyone's viewpoint change? Why? Why not?

Extended Learning:

Invite students to research a controversial issue that you are interested in. Obtain evidence for both sides. Next, students should create a Popplet graphic organizer to display both sides of the argument.

Notes:

_____

_____

_____

_____

_____

Drawing Dictations

(ABOUT 40 MINUTES)

Common Core:
CCSS.ELA-LITERACY.SL.6-8.4
Present claims and findings,
sequencing ideas logically and using
pertinent descriptions, facts, and
details to accentuate main ideas or
themes; use appropriate eye
contact, adequate volume, and
clear pronunciation.

CCSS.ELA-LITERACY.W.6-8.3
Write narratives to develop real or
imagined experiences or events
using effective technique, relevant
descriptive details, and well-
structured event sequences.

21st Century Skills:
Communication, Media Literacy,
Leadership and Responsibility

ISTE/NETS:
Communication and collaboration B

Technology operations and
concepts D

Leadership & Responsibility:

Student leaders can effectively speak and listen.

Objective:

Students will be able to create a replica of a diagram with a partner by using effective oral communication skills. Students will be able to discuss effective speaking and listening.

Materials:

Note cards, markers.

Steps:

- Pass out note cards and markers to each student. Ask students to create a diagram with various shapes, lines, letters, and numbers.
- Collect and shuffle cards.
- Next, have students form pairs and sit back to back. Determine Partner A and Partner B.
- Partner A will have a blank paper and markers. Partner B will have a diagram. Partner B should describe the diagram to his partner who will try to draw what she hears. Partner A cannot talk or ask questions.
- Partners then need to compare diagrams and get ready to switch roles. For the second round tell students the person drawing can now talk. Encourage partners to come up with a strategy for getting an accurate drawing. For example, students can decide they will ask each other questions and be more specific.
- Next, hand out a second diagram and have pairs repeat the exercise. Invite pairs to share pictures.
- Allow partners to show their diagrams. Have the whole group discuss their strategies and what helped with their communication.

Personal Reflection:

- Write about a time when you had to use effective speaking skills.
- Write about a time when you had to use effective listening skills.

Group Reflection:

- What helped improve communication from the first to second round? What did each person do differently?
- As leaders in a school community, what can we do to help make sure we are being understood when we speak? What can we do to make sure we understand when we listen?
- What kind of a communicator should a student leader be? Can a student be a quiet, introverted leader?
- What makes a leader an effective communicator?
- Why do you think some students don't voice their opinions and ideas?

Source: Photo by Julie Hellerstein.

Extended Learning:

Students can practice their communication skills by using the ShowMe app and draw or describe a picture. Using the ShowMe app, students can draw a caricature of an effective leader and describe his or her characteristics and communication skills.

Notes:

_____

_____

_____

_____

_____

From Here to There Worksheet

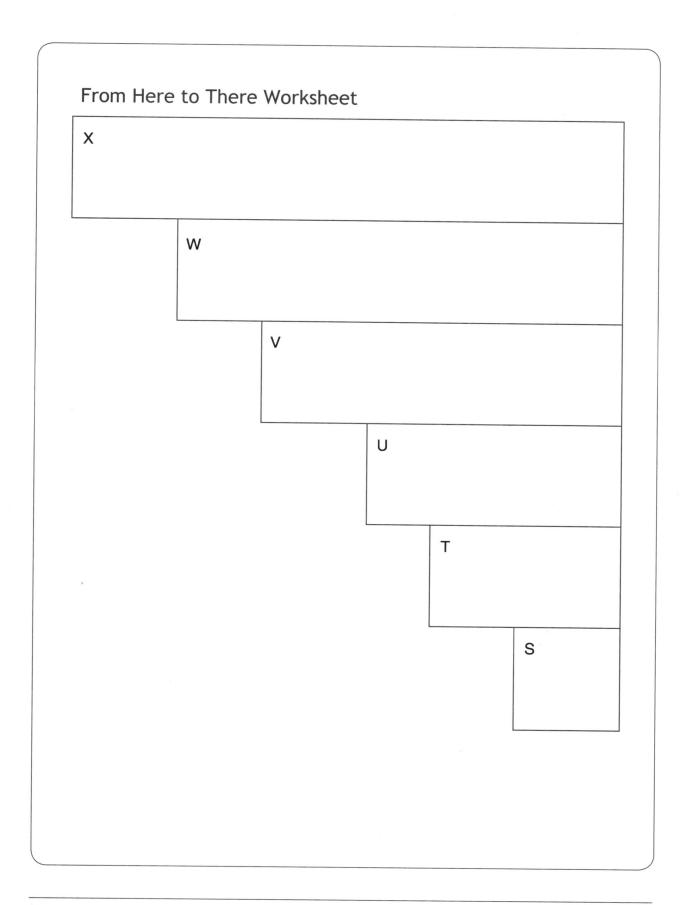

X

W

V

U

T

S

Using the graphic organizer's content, students should create an interactive Prezi to show how they get from "There" to "Here." Encourage students to display information creatively. Create an interactive Prezi, map, or timeline. Students should use pictures and multimedia to showcase their plan.

Notes:

_____

_____

_____

_____

_____

_____

_____

_____

_____

_____

_____

_____

Linked-In Learning

(ABOUT 50 MINUTES, FOLLOW-UP ON SUBSEQUENT DAYS)

Confidence to Take Action:

Confidence to Take Action is about dreaming about the future and doing something in the present to reach those dreams.

Objective:

Students will be able to create and design a LinkedIn profile to showcase their achievements and make relevant connections in their field of interest.

Materials:

Computer or device with Internet access; LinkedIn website.

Steps:

- Discuss the purpose of networking and professional online etiquette. Why is it important to build professional connections? Prior to the lesson, review online safety and digital citizenship.

- Explain to students that they will be building a LinkedIn profile.

- Students should create a profile based on their personal information and achievements. This is similar to building a resume. Students can write about their work experience, projects, education, honors and awards, courses, certifications, languages, organizations, volunteer work, and more! Allow students to bring in records, grades, and relevant documents to help them complete these sections. Students can also bring in a resume if they have written one for another class or job.

- While drafting their profiles, students should research and consider using industry-specific terminology. Share a list of resume words that highlight different skills.

Common Core:
CCSS.ELA-LITERACY.W.9-12.6
Use technology, including the Internet, to produce, publish, and update individual or shared writing products, taking advantage of technology's capacity to link to other information and to display information flexibly and dynamically.

CCSS.ELA-LITERACY.W.9-12.10
Write routinely over extended time frames (time for research, reflection, and revision) and shorter time frames (a single sitting or a day or two) for a range of tasks, purposes, and audiences.

21st Century Skills:
Critical Thinking and Problem Solving, Initiative and Self-Direction, Leadership and Responsibility

ISTE/NETS:
Technology operations and concepts A

Critical thinking, problem solving, and decision making C

Communication and collaboration A, B

Research and information fluency A, B

- Allow students to view other LinkedIn profiles in their industry of choice. Have students search for the job of their choice under the Jobs tab. For example, a student could type in sales representative. Students can scan through some of the key skills and experience that the employers are looking for in a sales representative. Students may also search and look at different profiles of people in their future industry or their connections. Exploring the website will allow students to get a sense of how to network and a snapshot of what the job industry looks like!

- Next, allow students to explore. Students can search for employers, industry influencers and personal connections to add to their network. Students can also follow businesses and companies of their choice. Allow students to follow a channel on the new LinkedIn Pulse section. They can also job search by location. Encourage students to join LinkedIn Groups, follow university pages of schools they are interested in attending.

- Students should discuss what makes a candidate stand out with a partner. How many skill endorsements do they have? Does it appear that this person is active on LinkedIn? Do they have over 500 connections? What accomplishments stand out?

- Students may add and edit their profiles as they learn new strategies, terminology, and ideas.

- Next, students should add each other as connections to start building their network. Encourage students to endorse each other honestly for different skills. For example, a student on the prom-planning committee could be endorsed for Event Planning. Encourage students to take this seriously and not just endorse each other because they are friends.

- Students can also share relevant articles related to their future field of choice and contribute to the professional learning network!

Students should debrief the experience by writing or verbally explaining three interesting things they learned from using LinkedIn about the industry or career they selected. Students can describe their experience with building their profile, exploring, and connecting.

Personal Reflection:

- Students can also share relevant articles related to their future field of choice and contribute to the professional learning network! Students should debrief the experience by writing or verbally explaining three interesting things they learned from using LinkedIn about the industry or career selected.

- Students can describe their experience with building their profile, exploring, and connecting.

Group Reflection:

- In small groups, students should discuss the following: What was the most useful thing you learned about the industry or career you selected? Why is it important to build professional connections? What does it mean to network?

- How can networking help you gain Confidence to Take Action in achieving your goals? What is it like to promote your skills and accomplishments? What is your greatest asset? How does it help you now? How will this asset help you in the future?

Extended Learning:

Assign students the task of marketing themselves by making a short advertisement using the technology of their choice. Encourage students to be creative as they think about how they can best sell their skills and strengths. Bring in a guest recruiter to give feedback on the marketing pitches.

Invite professionals from a variety of industries to Skype or video call with your class. Students should prepare questions before the video call!

Notes:
_____

_____

_____

_____

_____

_____

_____

_____

_____

_____

_____

Cool, Calm, and Confident Collage

(ABOUT 30 MINUTES)

Common Core:

CCSS.ELA-LITERACY.W.9-12.3
Write narratives to develop real or imagined experiences or events using effective technique, well-chosen details, and well-structured event sequences.

CCSS.ELA-LITERACY.SL.9-12.1
Initiate and participate effectively in a range of collaborative discussions (one-on-one, in groups, and teacher-led) with diverse partners on grades 9-12 topics, texts, and issues, building on others' ideas and expressing their own clearly and persuasively.

21st Century Skills:
Creativity and Innovation, Communication, Initiative and Self-Direction

ISTE/NETS:
Creativity and innovation B
Digital citizenship B, C, D,
Technology operations and concepts A, B, D

Confidence to Take Action:

Confidence to Take Action is about believing in yourself and your abilities. This activity helps students tap into times they felt extremely confident in what they were doing.

Objective:

Students will be able to identify and reflect on an experience when they were very confident.

Materials:

Devices with PicCollage or Pic Stitch app; or magazines, pictures, paper, scissors.

Steps:

- Warm-up discussion: What does it mean to be self-confident? What are you confident about?
- Invite students to take a trip down "Memory Lane"! Some might travel back further than others, but everyone, at some time, has felt self-confident.
- Ask students to consider a time they felt very confident in what they were doing. The memory might relate to school, sports, music, a hobby, or even a relationship.
- Allow students to brainstorm. Students can look through pictures, past social media posts, and other artifacts for ideas! Collect items for the collage.
- Have students make a collage (digital or paper) of that memory. The collage does not need to be literal. Encourage students to be abstract and creative.
- Have students share their creations in small groups or with the whole class if time permits.

Personal Reflection:

- What does it feel like to be self-confident?
- What activity or event would you like to be as confident in as you depicted in your collage?
- How could you tap into previous experiences of acting with confidence today?

Group Reflection:

- What role does self-confidence play in a healthy life?
- Why is it important to recognize your strengths?
- Reflect on someone who boosts your confidence. What specifically does this person do to make you feel good about who you are and what you are doing?
- What are some ways you could boost your own confidence? Brainstorm a list of self-confidence improving actions: help coach an elementary sports team, tutor another student, keep a journal of your accomplishments.
- What are some small things students could do everyday that would positively affect others' confidence? Share your ideas with peers.

Extended Learning:

Watch pep talk from Kid President at https://www.youtube.com/watch?v=l-gQLqv9f4o. Write a pep talk to yourself to follow your dreams. Create an Internet meme, video, or visual aid to go along with your pep talk.

Notes:

_____

_____

_____

_____

_____

_____

_____

Time Capsule

(ABOUT 50 MINUTES)

Common Core:
CCSS.ELA-LITERACY.W.6.10

Write routinely over extended time frames (time for research, reflection, and revision) and shorter time frames (a single sitting or a day or two) for a range of discipline-specific tasks, purposes, and audiences.

21st Century Skills:
Creativity and Innovation, Collaboration, Social and Cross-Cultural Interaction

ISTE/NETS:
Research and information fluency B

Creativity and innovation B, D

Communication and collaboration D

Digital citizenship A, B

Confidence to Take Action:

Confidence to Take Action is about thinking of your future and doing something to make that future happen.

Objective:

Students will be able to reflect on their confidence and accomplishments by creating a personal time capsule that they will revisit at the end of the school year.

Materials:

One container for each student—containers should be the size of a small box (e.g., a small can, coffee can); time capsule sheet; decorating materials.

Steps:

- Warm-up discussion: What does it mean to be confident? What does it mean to be proud of you who and what you are doing? What do you hope to accomplish by the end of the year?

- Have students create a *K-W-L* chart and research on time capsules. Find relevant articles to frame the activity. For example, have students read articles about the 1795 time capsule found in Boston (Samuel Adams and Paul Revere).

- Let students know that they are going to be putting together their own time capsule. Ask students what type of items might go in a time capsule and why.

- Give each student a time capsule container to decorate.

- Students should fill out the time capsule worksheet.

- Next, have students put at least five things in the time capsule: the time capsule worksheet, a piece of writing or artwork, and three things that represent them now. Students may need to bring these items from home so plan accordingly with due dates.

- Have students seal the time capsules and put them away until the end of the year.

- At the end of the year, open the time capsules and let students share their items as well as how they have grown over the course of the year.

- This activity can be done for short-term goals as well. Time capsules can be put away for a month or several months.

Time Capsule Worksheet

1. What is today's date?

2. What is the weather like today?

3. What specifically are you wearing today?

4. What songs have you most recently listened to?

5. What just happened on your favorite TV show or book that you are currently reading?

6. What is your funniest or happiest recent memory?

7. Describe the person you are today.

8. What is your personal motto or philosophy?

9. List a few things you hope to learn over the course of the year.

10. How do you hope to grow personally by the end of the school year?

11. What do you hope your friends will say about you at the end of the year?

12. What do you think will be your biggest challenge this year?

13. Describe a recent accomplishment.

14. What are your life goals at the moment?

15. What will some of your successes be?

Personal Reflection:

- After making the time capsule: What was it like to visualize your goals and dreams? How important is it to think about your future?

- At the end of the year: What surprised you most about your time capsule? What have you accomplished since your time capsule? How have you changed? What has stayed the same?

Group Reflection:

Develop a time capsule that represents what it means to be a student at your school in the current year. Write letters to the future students and encourage students to be confident. Bury it and decide a date when it can be opened—for example, for a social studies class to open in the year 2045.

Extended Learning:

Students who are over 13 years old: Timehop is an app that gives you a daily feed of your old photos, Facebook, Twitter, Instagram, and camera roll photos. Have students create new material for their future selves to post today that will go into their Timehop the next year. Next, have students reflect on their past social media posts. Discuss digital citizenship. Have students write and reflect on past memories.

Students who are under 13 years old: Review pictures from the past on your device. Do you see any pictures where you had a lot of self-confidence? How could you tap into previous experiences of acting with confidence today? Discuss digital citizenship.

Source: Courtesy of Timehop.

Extreme Community Makeover

(ABOUT 50 MINUTES)

Confidence to Take Action:

Confidence to Take Action is about making a difference in the school, community, and world. All students can dream about and act upon what differences they can make.

Objective:

Students will be able to create a plan of action for a cause they believe in.

Materials:

Materials may vary depending on student projects; most will need devices or computers with Internet access.

Steps:

- Put students in groups of three or four.
- Let students know they are going to have an opportunity to build a better community.
- Students should begin by brainstorming their ideal community. What would be different? Why?
- Allow students to research community transformation projects from other cities.
- After brainstorming, students will represent their new community through pictures, social media posts, Minecraft or a build-a-city video game or app, videos, stories, a collage, or other display that represents their vision.
- Next, students will research or write a proposal of a small change they could take to work toward this vision.
- Allow enough time for students to share their visions. If possible, invite community leaders to hear the final projects.

Personal Reflection:

- How can you take action to improve your community?
- What other areas of your life would you like to make a change? What action steps will you take? What do you expect the outcome to be?

> **Common Core:**
> CCSS.ELA-LITERACY.W.6-8.7
> Conduct short research projects to answer a question, drawing on several sources and refocusing the inquiry when appropriate.
>
> **21st Century Skills:**
> Critical Thinking and Problem Solving, Creativity and Innovation, Collaboration
>
> **ISTE/NETS:**
> Research and information fluency A
> Communication and collaboration A, D
> Creativity and innovation A, B, C, D

Group Reflection:

- How can small acts make a big difference?
- Can people of all ages make a difference in their communities?
- How does making a difference feel?

Extended Learning:

Internet memes have the potential to go viral! Visit Project MASH and have students create and track an Internet meme about a change they would like to see in their community or in the world. Visit http://alpha.projectmash.org/experience/change-your-meme for more information.

Notes:

_____

_____

_____

_____

_____

_____

_____

_____

_____

_____

_____

_____

Letter to the Editor

(ABOUT 50 MINUTES)

Confidence to Take Action:

Confidence to Take Action can involve persuading others to take up a cause you believe in.

Objective:

Students will be able to write a persuasive editorial piece regarding a current event or relevant issue.

Materials:

Editorial pages from newspaper, magazines, or online sites.

Steps:

- Explain that one effective way to have your opinion and ideas heard is to write a letter to the editor. Many people read editorial pages of newspapers or magazines, and often a letter or e-mail to the editor will shine light on an important issue. In this activity, students will be asked to write letters to the editor about an issue that concerns them.

- Have students read a variety of editorials from online sources. Visit the *New York Times* student editorial contest at http://nyti.ms/1tyLeyW. Ask: What are your thoughts on the editorials? Do they agree with them? What makes a good editorial?

- Inform your students that they are going to write a letter to the editor about an issue that concerns them that was brought up in a recent issue of the newspaper or magazine. First, students should find an article to form an opinion on or students can select a topic first and then choose the newspaper or magazine that best fits the topic.

- Compile the student letters into a classroom blog or forum.

- Have students read and respond to each other's editorials.

- Have students find e-mail addresses to the editor of the publications and mail them. Be sure to keep a watch for students' letters being published.

> **Common Core:**
> CCSS.ELA-LITERACY.W.6.1
> Write arguments to support claims with clear reasons and relevant evidence.
>
> **21st Century Skills:**
> Communication, Media Literacy, Critical Thinking and Problem Solving
>
> **ISTE/NETS:**
> Communication and collaboration A, B
>
> Research and information fluency C
>
> Critical thinking, problem solving, and decision making C, D
>
> Digital citizenship A

Personal Reflection:

- What was it like to voice your opinion?
- When do you voice your opinion at school?
- When do you voice your opinion in life? Give examples.
- Write a letter to your principal about an issue that matters to the class or you personally.

Group Reflection:

- Why do people read editorials?
- What constitutes a good editorial?
- Why is it important for students to voice their opinions?
- How do students have voice at school?

Extended Learning:

Have students voice their opinions about movies. Go to www.rottentomatoes.com. What constitutes a good review? Read several critic reviews and user reviews. Write a review on a movie you have recently watched in class or outside of school. How do you effectively voice your opinion online or in other forums?

Notes:

_____

_____

_____

_____

_____

_____

_____

_____

_____

Common Core State Standards, Grades 6–12

	BELONGING		HEROES		SENSE OF ACCOMPLISHMENT		FUN & EXCITEMENT		CURIOSITY & CREATIVITY		SPIRIT OF ADVENTURE		LEADERSHIP & RESPONSIBILITY		CONFIDENCE TO TAKE ACTION	
	9-12	6-8	9-12	6-8	9-12	6-8	9-12	6-8	9-12	6-8	9-12	6-8	9-12	6-8	9-12	6-8
CCSS.ELA–LITERACY.CCRA.W.3	X				X						X					
CCSS.ELA–LITERACY.W.9-10.6	X		X						X				X		X	
CCSS.ELA–LITERACY.SL.9-10.1	X				X						X		X		X	
CCSS.ELA–LITERACY.SL.11-12.1	X							X			X		X		X	
CCSS.ELA–LITERACY.SL.6.1		X				X		X		X				X		X
CCSS.ELA–LITERACY.SL.7.1		X				X		X		X				X		X
CCSS.ELA–LITERACY.SL.8.1		X				X				X				X		X
CCSS.ELA–LITERACY.W.6.6		X				X										
CCSS.ELA–LITERACY.W.7.6		X														
CCSS.ELA–LITERACY.W.8.6		X														
CCSS.ELA–LITERACY.CCRA.W 4		X		X		X	X									
CCSS.ELA–LITERACY.CCRA.W 6		X		X			X					X			X	
CCSS.ELA–LITERACY.W.9-10.2.B			X													
CCSS.ELA–LITERACY.W.9-12.3			X										X		X	
CCSS.ELA–LITERACY.W.9-10.2.A			X													
CCSS.ELA–LITERACY.RI.9-10.1			X													
CCSS.ELA–LITERACY.RI.7.1				X												
CCSS.ELA–LITERACY.CCRA.R.7				X												

(Continued)

	BELONGING		HEROES		SENSE OF ACCOMPLISHMENT		FUN & EXCITEMENT		CURIOSITY & CREATIVITY		SPIRIT OF ADVENTURE		LEADERSHIP & RESPONSIBILITY		CONFIDENCE TO TAKE ACTION	
	9-12	6-8	9-12	6-8	9-12	6-8	9-12	6-8	9-12	6-8	9-12	6-8	9-12	6-8	9-12	6-8
CCSS.ELA–LITERACY.RI.9-10.6					X											
CCSS.ELA–LITERACY.RI.11-12.5					X											X
CCSS.ELA–LITERACY.W.6.2						X										
CCSS.ELA–LITERACY.W.6.4						X						X		X		X
CCSS.ELA–LITERACY.W.6.5						X										
CCSS.ELA–LITERACY.W.9-10.4							X									
CCSS.ELA–LITERACY.W.9-10.6							X									
CCSS.ELA–LITERACY.SL.9-10.5							X				X		X			
CCSS.ELA–LITERACY.SL.8.4								X				X		X		
CCSS.ELA–LITERACY.W.11-12.3									X		X		X			X
CCSS.ELA–LITERACY.W.HST.7									X	X						X
CCSS.ELA–LITERACY.W.6-8.10										X						
CCSS.ELA–LITERACY.SL.7.4												X		X		
CCSS.ELA–LITERACY.SL.6-8.5												X				
CCSS.ELA–LITERACY.W.6-8.2												X				
CCSS.ELA–LITERACY.W.9-12.10													X		X	
CCSS.ELA–LITERACY.W.6-8.3														X		

Partnership for 21st Century Skills, Grades 6–12

	BELONGING		HEROES		SENSE OF ACCOMPLISHMENT		FUN & EXCITEMENT		CURIOSITY & CREATIVITY		SPIRIT OF ADVENTURE		LEADERSHIP & RESPONSIBILITY		CONFIDENCE TO TAKE ACTION	
	9-12	6-8	9-12	6-8	9-12	6-8	9-12	6-8	9-12	6-8	9-12	6-8	9-12	6-8	9-12	6-8
Critical Thinking and Problem Solving	X	X	X		X	X	X	X	X	X	X		X	X	X	X
Creativity and Innovation			X	X	X	X	X	X	X	X	X	X	X		X	X
Communication	X	X	X	X	X	X	X	X			X	X		X		X
Collaboration	X	X	X	X	X	X	X	X		X	X	X	X	X		X
Information Literacy	X							X							X	
Media Literacy	X	X	X			X	X	X						X	X	X
ICT Literacy	X	X	X				X								X	
Flexibility and Adaptability											X					
Initiative and Self-Direction						X	X		X	X	X	X	X			X
Social and Cross-Cultural Interaction	X											X				X
Productivity and Accountability						X			X	X		X				
Leadership and Responsibility				X							X		X	X	X	

ISTE Standards, Grades 6–12

	BELONGING		HEROES		SENSE OF ACCOMPLISHMENT		FUN & EXCITEMENT		CURIOSITY & CREATIVITY		SPIRIT OF ADVENTURE		LEADERSHIP & RESPONSIBILITY		CONFIDENCE TO TAKE ACTION	
	9-12	6-8	9-12	6-8	9-12	6-8	9-12	6-8	9-12	6-8	9-12	6-8	9-12	6-8	9-12	6-8
1. Creativity and Innovation A	X	X	X	X			X	X	X	X	X	X				X
1. Creativity and Innovation B	X	X	X	X	X	X	X	X	X	X	X	X	X			X
1. Creativity and Innovation C		X					X						X			X
1. Creativity and Innovation D	X	X	X				X	X								X
2. Communication and Collaboration A	X	X	X	X			X	X	X	X						X
2. Communication and Collaboration B	X	X	X	X	X	X	X	X				X	X	X		X
2. Communication and Collaboration C		X					X									
2. Communication and Collaboration D	X	X	X	X	X	X	X	X	X	X				X		X
3. Research and Information Fluency A	X	X	X	X					X			X			X	
3. Research and Information Fluency B	X	X	X	X	X				X	X				X	X	X
3. Research and Information Fluency C	X	X	X						X	X				X	X	
3. Research and Information Fluency D	X	X	X						X	X			X		X	
4. Critical Thinking, Problem Solving, and Decision Making A	X							X	X	X			X		X	

	BELONGING		HEROES		SENSE OF ACCOMPLISHMENT		FUN & EXCITEMENT		CURIOSITY & CREATIVITY		SPIRIT OF ADVENTURE		LEADERSHIP & RESPONSIBILITY		CONFIDENCE TO TAKE ACTION	
	9-12	6-8	9-12	6-8	9-12	6-8	9-12	6-8	9-12	6-8	9-12	6-8	9-12	6-8	9-12	6-8
4. Critical Thinking, Problem Solving, and Decision Making B			X					X	X	X	X				X	
4. Critical Thinking, Problem Solving, and Decision Making C							X	X	X	X				X	X	
4. Critical Thinking, Problem Solving, and Decision Making D					X			X	X	X	X		X	X	X	
5. Digital Citizenship A							X	X			X				X	X
5. Digital Citizenship B		X	X	X			X	X			X	X			X	X
5. Digital Citizenship C							X				X				X	
5. Digital Citizenship D							X				X				X	
6. Technology Operations and Concepts A		X	X				X						X		X	
6. Technology Operations and Concepts B			X				X	X			X		X		X	
6. Technology Operations and Concepts C							X								X	
6. Technology Operations and Concepts D		X					X							X	X	

Index

Accomplishment. *See* Sense of
Accomplishment
Action. *See* Confidence to Take Action
Act It Out, 57
Adventure. *See* Spirit of Adventure
Adventure Advice, 93–94
Adventure Challenge, 90
Advice activities:
Adventure Advice, 93–94
Good, Bad, Horrible Advice,
105–107
All About Me Cloud and Class Cloud,
16–17
Appy Hour, 63–64
Aspirations, xi, xii–xiii, xii (figure)
Aspirations Framework, xiii
Aspirations Profile, xi–xiii, xii (figure)
Aspirations Story Squares, 3–6

Barlas, Meral, 76
Belonging:
about, xiv, 1–2
All About Me Cloud and Class
Cloud, 16–17
Aspirations Story Squares, 3–6
Belong-Meme, 18–19
Inside/Outside, 10–11
Odd Dot Out, 7–9
Pick a Number, 12–15
Belong-Meme, 18–19
Big Event, The, 57
Blackout Poetry, 69–71
Board games, 65–66
Breaking News, 22–23

Card games, 65–66
Challenge zone, 83
Change in the Cafeteria, The, 114
Cheater Cross Country, 114
Class Dojo system, 40, 51, 51 (figure)
Clubs, 1
Collages, 124
Comfort zone, 83
Conditions, overview of, xiv–xv
See also specific conditions
Confidence to Take Action:
about, xv, 115–116
Cool, Calm, and Confident Collage,
124–125
Extreme Community Makeover,
129–130
Letter to the Editor, 131–132
Linked-In Learning, 121–123

From There to Here, 117–120
Time Capsule, 126–128
Cool, Calm, and Confident Collage,
124–125
Creativity. *See* Curiosity & Creativity
Curiosity & Creativity:
about, xiv, 67–68
Blackout Poetry, 69–71
Curiosity Convention, The, 79–80
Genius Hour/Passion Project, 72–74
Marshmallow Challenge, 81–82
Quick Question, 77–78
Why Do We Need to
Learn This?, 75–76
Curiosity Convention, The, 79–80

Davidson, Tinney, 27
Detention (scenario), 114
Drawing Dictations, 110–111

Editorials, 131–132
Edmodo, 44, 64, 106, 113–114
8 Conditions, overview of, xiv–xv
See also specific conditions
Einstein, Albert, 80
*Elderly Woman Waves at Students
Every Day. Then She Got a HUGE
Surprise*, 27
Engagement, xiii, xiv
See also Curiosity & Creativity;
Fun & Excitement; Spirit of
Adventure
Excitement. *See* Fun & Excitement
Extreme Community Makeover,
129–130
Extreme Lesson Make Over, 55

Famous Failures, 44
Flipped classrooms, 115
From There to Here, 117–120
Fun & Excitement:
about, xiv, 52–53
Appy Hour, 63–64
Heads Up!, 61–62
Learning That Sticks, 59–60
Menu, 56–58
Tweet Teach, 54–55
Un-Bored Games, 65–66

"Genius Bar Goes to School-
Generation YES," 85
Genius Bars, 85–86
Genius Hour/Passion Project, 72–74

Good, Bad, Horrible Advice, 105–107
Google Nexus TV commercial, 91
Gossip Girls and Guys, 114
Grades 6–8 Belonging activities:
All About Me Cloud and
Class Cloud, 16–17
Belong-Meme, 18–19
Pick a Number, 12–15
Grades 6–8 Confidence to Take Action
activities:
Extreme Community Makeover,
129–130
Letter to the Editor, 131–132
Time Capsule, 126–128
Grades 6–8 Curiosity & Creativity
activities:
Curiosity Convention, The, 79–80
Marshmallow Challenge, 81–82
Quick Question, 77–78
Grades 6–8 Fun & Excitement
activities:
Appy Hour, 63–64
Heads Up!, 61–62
Un-Bored Games, 65–66
Grades 6–8 Heroes activities:
Gratitude, 33–34
I Can Be a Hero Poem, 29–30
Utilizing YOU!, 31–32
Grades 6–8 Leadership &
Responsibility activities:
Drawing Dictations, 110–111
Tag Team Debate, 108–109
Values Auction, 112–114
Grades 6–8 Sense of Accomplishment
activities:
Headline News, 49–51
Marble Roll, 43–44
Student Actions, 45–48
Grades 6–8 Spirit of Adventure
activities:
Adventure Advice, 93–94
Never Lose Sight of Your Goal, 95–96
Student Speak, 91–92
Grades 9–12 Belonging activities:
Aspirations Story Squares, 3–6
Inside/Outside, 10–11
Odd Dot Out, 7–9
Grades 9–12 Confidence to Take
Action activities:
Cool, Calm, and Confident
Collage, 124–125
Linked-In Learning, 121–123
From There to Here, 117–120

Grades 9–12 Curiosity & Creativity activities:
  Blackout Poetry, 69–71
  Genius Hour/Passion Project, 72–74
  Why Do We Need to Learn This?, 75–76
Grades 9–12 Fun & Excitement activities:
  Learning That Sticks, 59–60
  Menu, 56–58
  Tweet Teach, 54–55
Grades 9–12 Heroes activities:
  Breaking News, 22–23
  Heroes-Based Learning, 27–28
  Heroes Here in the Classroom, 24–26
Grades 9–12 Leadership & Responsibility activities:
  Good, Bad, Horrible Advice, 105–107
  Scholarship Situations, 99–101
  School Solutions, 102–104
Grades 9–12 Sense of Accomplishment activities:
  Scholarship, 37–38
  Snapshot Show and Tell, 41–42
  What About the Rest of the Alphabet?, 39–40
Grades 9–12 Spirit of Adventure activities:
  I Dare You Cards, 89–90
  Student-Led Help Desk, 85–86
  In the Zone, 87–88
Graphic organizers, 3–6
Gratitude, 33–34
Guiding Principles, xiii–xiv

Headline News, 49–51
Heads Up!, 61–62
Help desks, 85–86
Heroes:
  about, xiv, 20–21
  Breaking News, 22–23
  Gratitude, 33–34
  Heroes-Based Learning, 27–28
  Heroes Here in the Classroom, 24–26
  I Can Be a Hero Poem, 29–30
  Utilizing YOU!, 31–32
Heroes-Based Learning, 27–28
Heroes Here in the Classroom, 24–26
Heroes Young Wonder: Joshua Williams, 30
Hibernation, xii, xii (figure)
Hyperlapse app, 60

I Can Be a Hero Poem, 29–30
I Dare You Cards, 89–90
Imaginary Field Trip, 57
Imagination, xii, xii (figure)
Inside/Outside, 10–11
Interdisciplinary work, 67
Internet memes, 18–19, 130
In the Zone, 87–88
iPad, The (scenario), 114

Josephine Hart Poetry App, 29

Keller, Helen, 83
Kid President's Pep Talk to Teachers and Students!, 73, 80
Kleon, Austin, 69
K-W-L charts, 31–32, 126

Leadership & Responsibility:
  about, xiv, 97–98
  Drawing Dictations, 110–111
  Good, Bad, Horrible Advice, 105–107
  Scholarship Situations, 99–101
  School Solutions, 102–104
  Tag Team Debate, 108–109
  Values Auction, 112–114
Learning That Sticks, 59–60
Letter to the Editor, 131–132
Linked-In Learning, 121–123

MAAP. *See* My Aspirations Action Plan
Maiers, Angela, 80
Marble Roll, 43–44
Marshmallow Challenge, 81–82
Memes, 18–19, 130
Menu, 56–58
Mind maps, 78
Movie-Making Madness, 56
Movie reviews, 132
My Aspirations Action Plan (MAAP), 118

Never Lose Sight of Your Goal, 95–96
News activities:
  Breaking News, 22–23
  Headline News, 49–51
New York Times, 37

Odd Dot Out, 7–9

Panic zone, 84
Peer review boards, 97
Perspiration, xii, xii (figure)
Pick a Number, 12–15
Pinterest, 71
Poetry activities:
  Blackout Poetry, 69–71
  I Can Be a Hero Poem, 29–30
Popplet app, 78, 109
Prezi, 75, 120
Project MASH, 130
Public speaking, 91–92
Purpose, xiii–xiv, xiv–xv
  See also Confidence to Take Action; Leadership & Responsibility

Quick Question, 77–78

Remix, 57
Report cards, 35
Responsibility. *See* Leadership & Responsibility
Robotics class, 83
Rotten Tomatoes website, 132

Scenarios, school, 114
Scholarship, 37–38
Scholarship Situations, 99–101
School Solutions, 102–104
Self-Worth, xiii, xiv
  See also Belonging; Heroes; Sense of Accomplishment
Sense of Accomplishment:
  about, xiv, 35–36
  Headline News, 49–51
  Marble Roll, 43–44
  Scholarship, 37–38
  Snapshot Show and Tell, 41–42
  Student Actions, 45–48
  What About the Rest of the Alphabet?, 39–40
Snap cups, 50
Snapshot Show and Tell, 41–42
Social Media Student Suspension, 114
Spirit of Adventure:
  about, xiv, 83–84
  Adventure Advice, 93–94
  I Dare You Cards, 89–90
  Never Lose Sight of Your Goal, 95–96
  Student-Led Help Desk, 85–86
  Student Speak, 91–92
  In the Zone, 87–88
Student Actions, 45–48
Student-Led Help Desk, 85–86
Student Speak, 91–92

Tag Team Debate, 56, 108–109
Teaching, 52
Thank-you cards, 33
Theme Party, 57
3 Guiding Principles, xiii–xiv
Time Capsule, 126–128
Timehop app, 128, 128 (figure)
TouchCast app, 23
"Tuition Aid From a Zombie Elf," 37
Tweet Teach, 54–55
Twitter, 54–55, 73

Un-Bored Games, 65–66
Utilizing YOU!, 31–32

Values Auction, 112–114
Visual Discovery, 56

What About the Rest of the Alphabet?, 39–40
"What Criteria Should Be Used in Awarding Scholarships for College?", 37
What Is Fair?, 114
Why Do We Need to Learn This?, 75–76
Williams, Joshua, 30
"Will I Ever Need to Know This in Real Life?" (Barlas), 76
Word clouds, 16–17, 77
Wordsalad, 16–17, 77, 78 (figure)

YouTube student video channel, 23

A SAGE Company

CORWIN HAS ONE MISSION: to enhance education through intentional professional learning.

We build long-term relationships with our authors, educators, clients, and associations who partner with us to develop and continuously improve the best evidence-based practices that establish and support lifelong learning.